EMERGING ENTREPRENEURSHIP AMONG SCHEDULED CASTES OF CONTEMPORARY INDIA

Emerging Entrepreneurship Among Scheduled Castes Of Contemporary India

A Study of Kolhapur City

S. M. DAHIWALE

CONCEPT PUBLISHING COMPANY, NEW DELHI-110059

The Indian Council of Social Science Research gave the financial support towards the publication of this book. However, the responsibility for the contents of the book, the facts stated, opinions expressed, conclusions reached, etc., in this book is entirely that of the author and not of the ICSSR.

ISBN 81-7022-261-3

First Published 1989

Samarth Modku **Dahiwale** (*b.* 1946-

Published by
Ashok Kumar Mittal
Concept Publishing Company
A/15-16, Commercial Block, Mohan Garden
NEW DELHI - 110059 (India)

Lasertypeset by
Microtech Advance Printing Systems (Pvt.) Ltd.
II-13, Bali Nagar, NEW DELHI-110015

Printed by
A. P. Offset,
1/11787 Panchsheel Garden,
Naveen Shahdara, Delhi 110 032.

Dedicated
to
the Memory of My Wife
the late Kunda

Preface

This present study is undertaken on the occupational mobility of ex-untouchables in self-employment sector. It has covered 230 respondents as sample from the five major castes; viz., Mahar, Mang, Dhor, Chambhar and Bhangi known in the Maharashtra region. The sample is restricted to Kolhapur City alone. The study is an attempt to examine the factors caused for both occupational and social mobility especially in the background of post-Independence mechanism of Constitutional commitment and historically the revolutionary changes brought about by the royal Shahu Chhatrapati of Kolhapur in the interests of the Scheduled Caste people.

The general tendency among the Scheduled Caste people is to choose the service jobs rather than self-employed jobs. It is quite natural for them since the opportunities are created due to the policy of reservation in the Service Sector. It has its own limitations of providing the service opportunities. Moreover, in future, sooner or later, there is possibility of scraping the principle of reservation from the Constitution. Considering both the facts, the best of alternative remains self-employment to the large number of people.

During the post-Independence period many of the age-old practices of caste and untouchability are not observed at least in the urban centres. A number of schemes and programmes of self-employment are coming up day-by-day and that are open to any one irrespective of one's caste, etc.. Due to such reasons also, I could get some 200 respondents from Kolhapur City having an occupational experience background of 27.6 years on an average in their self-employed modern occupational careers. Hence, I hope this study would be useful to the ex-untouchables in motivating them towards the adoption of self-employed jobs.

S.M. DAHIWALE

Acknowledgements

To carry out the present work, many people have helped me. I wish to record my debts to all of them. But, it is not possible to mention them all. However, I must record some of them.

I am especially obliged to my research guide Dr. (Mrs) S.V. Kaldate for her painstaking scrutiny of the drafts of my thesis. I am grateful to Dr. S.N. Pawar for his valuable suggestions in recording the data reported by the respondents and his time-to-time help for the completion of research work. I am thankful to Dr. Vilas Sangave, and Dr. R.K. Hebsur (TISS) for their guidance in the preparation and finalization of the Interview Schedule. My sincere thanks to Dr. S.P. Punalekar, Dr. R.B. Patil, Dr. J.B. Ambekar and P.B. Draxe whose suggestions and help regarding the references caused to a fruition. I am also obliged to my colleague D. Shrikant for suggesting the important modifications in the script.

To approach and contact the respondents for interview purpose Shivaji Ghatage, J.K. Kawale, Prakash Jamadagni and from the respondents Chandrakant Bhosale, Dr. L.R. Vhatakar and Akurdekar (tailor) helped me a great deal. The respondents also cooperated with me. Without their help and cooperation, the collection of data from the respondents would not have been easy. I thank them all.

I am thankful to Y.R. Tamhne and S.S. Patil of the Department of Archives, Kolhapur, for providing me the files relating Chhatrapati Shahu. My thanks to Rev. V.S. Kamble and Rev. Panhalkar for providing the literature on the origin and expansion of Christianity in the Kolhapur region. I must thank P.B. Patil, Regional Manager, Mahatma Phule Backward Class Development Corporation, Kolhapur, for making me available the list of beneficiaries of the financial assistance rendered by the corporation, Thanks to Pacherwal, C.S.I., and C.A. Mohite, the officers in the Kolhapur Municipal Corporation, for providing the figures needed for this work.

My thanks to the Tata Institute of Social Sciences, Bombay, for data processing, the Librarians of the University of Bombay, the

Tata Institute of Social Sciences, Bombay, and the University of Poona for providing source material and the facility for the study.

I am grateful to the University Grants Commission, New Delhi for financial assistance and to the Director, Western Regional Centre, Indian Council of Social Science Research, Bombay, for providing the facility of study-grant.

The author is grateful to the Indian Council of Social Science Research for the financial assistance for the publication of this thesis.

Department of Sociology
Shivaji University,
Kolhapur-416004

S.M. DAHIWALE

April 14, 1989

Contents

List of Tables

List of Plates

ONE

Theoretical Framework of the Study

In the light of the present study, theoretical perspectives are discussed here into two parts. The first deals with the explanations of occupational and purity-impurity notional sense of caste and untouchability along with the historical outline, and second, is referred to social mobility attributing to the modern encouraging factors such as anti-disabilities legislation and the introduction of open norms system such as democratic and secular values based on rational and scientific temper

I

HEREDITARY OCCUPATIONAL ROOTS OF CASTE AND UNTOUCHABILITY

Different theories are advanced to explain the development of caste system in India. Even today abandoning of job by a person from an ex-untouchable caste is not permitted. In India, it is observed especially more against the lowest untouchables. For the moment, if occupation is not considered as an explanation of caste, then why occupational restrictions are observed against the lower sections of the community in the region. This pertinent question takes us to the occupational origin of caste and untouchability. In spite of different origins of caste, an association between castes and occupations cannot be overlooked. Despite the controversies over the genesis of caste, occupational explanation is established by Ibbetson (1916), Karve (1958) and Ghurye (1969) considering the hereditary nature of caste.

Caste and Occupation

Ibbetson held: 'the fundamental idea which lay at the root of the institution in its inception was the hereditary nature of occupation'.[1]

Irawati Karve revealed association between caste and occupational structure closest by identifying some of the groups of occupational specialists and some caste designations indicating their occupations.[2] G.S. Ghurye too discerned 'lack of unrestricted choice of occupation' as one of the fundamental characteristics of caste system.[3] He elaborated: 'Generally a caste or a group of allied castes considered some of the callings as its hereditary occupation, to abandon which in pursuit of another, though it might be more lucrative, was thought not to be right. It was not only the moral restraint and the social check of one's caste-fellows that acted as a restraint on the choice of one's occupation, but also the restriction put by other castes, which did not allow member other than those of their own castes to follow their callings'.[4]

In support of the above occupational explanation of caste, a historical account based on Manu's prescriptives, proclamation of King Shivaji's policy towards the castes, and the present example of occupational disabilities indicating the role of traditional order is given in brief.

Occupational Prohibition to Sudras in Ancient India

To follow one's own hereditary occupation was regarded an ordained duty in ancient India according to the Shastras. Manu prescribed for Shudra 'to serve meekly upper three castes'.[5] If a man of low caste follows an occupation of a higher one, Manu laid down injunction that, 'the King shall deprive of his property and banish'.[6] In another place, Manu forbids 'Sudra from collection of wealth'. He laid down that, 'no collection of wealth must be made by a 'Sudra who has acquired wealth, gives pain to Brahmans'.[7] What is stated in 'the Laws of Manu' reveals the order of the ancient times.

Restoration of Caste During Shivaji Period

What Manu prescribed[8], King Shivaji restored the dharma in his Maratha country of Kolhapur and its adjacent region. Historically, A.D. 1630-1707, a period is known for Shivaji's rule. The king Shivaji in his Royal Order of January 28, A.D. 1677 made clear the policy towards the various castes: "The practices of each caste, as handed down by tradition, should be scrupulously observed. The Government would take prompt measures in full conformity with the shastras, traditions and customs, and without any prejudices against anyone, and after a careful scrutiny of the injunctions of the shastras, order the restoration of the Dharma or the appropriate practices'.[9] so it is clear by the proclamation that the king Shivaji was not against the restoration of traditional practices to be continued.

Caste Disabilities during the British Regime and Post-Independent India

What is stated in the Texts of the Shastras is found to be practised till today since ages together. Whether traditional order of caste is being restored even today can be revealed through the recent examples of Maharashtra and outside as well.

(1) In an examination before the Southborough Committee (1919)

Dr. Ambedkar had remembered 'a case in which a Mahar woman was taken to the police court for selling water-melons. In the Mills of Bombay Presidency the untouchables were not allowed to work in the weaving department; in one case an untouchable did work in the weaving department of a mill saying that he was a Mohammedan, and when found out, he was severely beaten'.[10]

(2) 'There are cases where some poor Brahmins who had taken to tailoring but have given it up because of the pressures exerted by their own caste men for accepting a religiously unsanctioned occupation leading to pollution, and by the caste tailors for entering their profession to oust the tailors from their tradition-bound occupation'.[11]

(3) 'When an immigrant Maratha (agricultural caste) man opened a laundry in a village near Poona assuming a different name, the dhobi (washerman's caste) men in the village vehemently protested against it as soon as they came to know that the owner was a Maratha. Dhobi caste men forced him to close down his shop and only the dhobis ran the laundries in this place'.[12]

(4) 'Caste Hindus, set on fire the house of Mukund Piraji, a Buddhist (Chikhali village, Dist.. Nanded) in which he incurred a loss of more than Rs. 3,000 in cash and other household belongings. He was running a fair price shop. Caste Hindus objected to the fair price shop in his name and approached the Government authorities to take it away from him and give to some caste Hindus. The govern-

ment authorities declined to do so. The upper caste-Hindus disliked this and did not buy the things from his shop due to untouchability'.[13]

(5) 'Caste Hindus armed with sticks, axe, spear, knives attacked Buddhists and looted their houses during night at 12 p.m. Afterwards, they burnt their huts. A cause reported was that the Government granted a piece of land for cultivation to the landless Buddhists of Chinchapur village, Tq. Sillod, Dt. Aurangabad'.[14]

(6) 'Caste Hindus grazed standing crops of Buddhists of Shiroli, Tq. Gangapur, Dt. Aurangabad. Cause reported was that Buddhists cultivated the lands to improve their economic conditions which was not liked by the caste Hindus'.[15]

(7) 'Caste-Hindus declared boycott on scheduled caste people on the instruction of village Sarpanch (head), village police Patil and other leaders. They stopped giving grains from the shops, did not give work to them, did not allow them to enter the lands and to pass through public roads. This incident occurred at Narayangaon village, Taluqa Paithan, Dt. Aurangabad. The cause was that, those scheduled caste people refused to do menial jobs'.[16]

(8) 'Buddhists of Bhadangwadi village (Dt. Bhir) received 225 acres of land from Government for their agricultural Cooperative society of which Mr.Sarpate was the chairman. This was not liked by the upper caste-Hindus, so they collectively attacked Mr. Sarpate and his associates with sticks and sharp weapons in which Mr. Sarpate and Mr. More were severely injured'.[17]

(9) 'Two scheduled caste persons were killed by high caste Hindus mercilessly when they were ploughing their fields. The cause was that they refused to remove the dead cattle. The incident occurred in Dekhwa village, Dt. Parbhani'.[18]

(10) Mr. D.D. Sonawane, who was Mahar, an untouchable by birth, converted to Buddhism, revealed his experience in Oct., 1978 on the occasion of Vijayadashmi festival of Hindus and also the day of conversion of Neo-Buddhists. What he *experienced in Pune City* is revealed in his words: "I opened a bakery shop by name Ajay. As there was no other bakery shop, it ran well. After some days my sister got married. Wedding ceremony was performed according to the Buddhist religion. I got identified by caste.[19] My bakery shop was put to loss. I found some customers asking me to put a piece of bread from distance. Customers stopped coming to my shop. I had to close down my bakery shop, because, I do not belong to the group of caste-Hindu or Christian or Muslim".[20]

(11) On the basis of the 10 villages each in Buldhana and Nasik Districts (Maharashtra), M.G. Kulkarni too concludes: 'Within the village such upward mobility has been still a difficult task for the scheduled castes to achieve'.[21]

(12) '... the Zamindari Abolition act passed by the Congress- controlled Uttar Pradesh Legislature in 1953... only four of the 6,000 acres of Khalapur land passed into the hands of the Untouchables.... Only two untouchables, one a Shoemaker, the other a Chamar, managed to gain little to land under this law and the Chamar was forced to sell his holding two years after its acquisition. This sale was brought about by various harrassments that culminated in the destruction of his crop by 'unknown' marauders shortly before harvest. Coercion of this kind and "hints' from powerful landlords finally forced him to sell his land to a Rajput neighbour'.[22]

It is evident that the order of the traditional India is found to be functional in both India of the British and the Republic. Moreover, it is clear through the above mentioned examples that even today mobility is not allowed to the members of the ex-untouchable castes in a village community. However, it is not forbidden in city but the *example of Pune* metropolitan in Maharashtra suggests that even in city, people from the ex-untouchable groups have to face their caste disabilities for mobility, however, to a lesser degree.

Occupational Mobility in Distress Permitted

In spite of the occupations prescribed by the laws of the Shastras to the four Varnas, Dutt quoted Shastras permitting downward occupational mobility to the upper three Varnas, viz., Brahman, Kshatriya, and Vaishya.[23] In addition to this, some injunctions are again found in Manusmriti permitting downward mobility to the upper Varnas[24]. However, a historian, Professor R.S. Sharma discussed the consequences upon the position of a person who had adopted lower occupations. To quote: "Baudhayan states that the Brahmanas who tend cattle, live by trade, work as artisans, actors, servants or usurers should be treated like Sudras. Gautama goes a step further and states that, if an arya adopts the occupations of non-aryan (i.e., a Sudra), he is reduced to his status'.[25]

With regard to the upward mobility of the lower castes, historian, Romila Thapar states: 'Instances of non-brahmanas being recruited to the rank of brahmanas are mentioned, but there are rare and are always referred to as something distinctly unusual'.[26]

It is clear that injunctions reveal the mobility permitted to the higher castes and not to the lowest/Sudras. However, there are exceptional examples of Valmiki Rishi and others whose origin is from Sudra but became Brahman. In contrast, there are other ancient examples whose mobility was prevented due to their caste disabilities. Sudra Shambuka who attempted to become enlightened by a devout austerity was decapitated by King Rama, and another example of Ekalavya who was prevented from becoming a master in archery. It indicates the act of preventing.

Despite the occupational explanation of caste in general, our immediate concern is with the hereditary nature of caste structure, and the restrictions imposed upon the persons of certain groups who have followed contemptuous occupations. Now, let us see, how the notion of untouchability developed too to prevent them from mobility.

PURITY-IMPURITY NOTIONAL ROOT OF UNTOUCHABILITY

In above, it is discussed that an occupation of a person is determined by the occupation of a caste to which one belongs. In the subsequent discussion, we have to see the religious origin of the notion of untouchability which is established since centuries together. In this background, Hocart long back had developed a religious explanation towards the notion of untouchability. Recently Dumont (1970) revived Hocart's explanation.[27] Hocart linked the caste and profession through the intermediary of religion.[28] Domont is pioneer to use the ideology of the pure and the impure to explain the notion of untouchability in caste system.

Impurity of Ex-Untouchable Caste

Domont does not claim the opposition between pure and impure as 'foundation' but states it 'central' for the society of caste.[29] He observes 'preoccupation with the pure and the impure is constant in Hindu life'.[30] In support of his observation he quotes a master of Sanskrit, Louis Renou that the notion of impurity 'is at the basis, theoretically at least, of the caste system'.....[31] Pure and impure opposition is observed by the members of each caste against one another in varying degrees. It is manifested in contrast exclusively between the caste-Hindus and the ex-untouchable castes. Dumont mentions the main features of untouchability, that : 'Untouchables have the job of disposing of the dead cattle of treating and working their skins'.[32] Ibbetson, too, had discussed the observance of the rules of purity-impurity, that; 'certain occupations shall be abstained from which are arbitrarily declared to be impure,... especially working on trading in leather and weaving; that impure food shall be avoided; that no communion shall be held with outcastes, such as scavengers, eaters of carrion or vormin, and the like'.[33] Ghurye also mentioned the ideas of purity, whether occupational or ceremonial to engender the practice of untouchability.[34]

Ex-Untouchables and Locality

The castes considered for the present study, especially, Mahar, Mang, Dhor, Chambhar and Bhangi are popularly known for their filthy jobs of menial services, making ropes and drumming skin objects, working with skins, scavenging and removing night soil. These jobs are regarded contemptuous. Those who deal with such jobs are segregated in their residential locality too. So the village is divided into two, viz., main village of caste Hindu people and the other outskirt of the ex-untouchables. In city also, the localities of ex-untouchable castes are easily identified. So the interplay between notion of *caste and locality* can be shown. Thus, Dumont's principle of hierarchy[35] is workable.

Hindu Religion and Untouchability

The religion of Hindu has played a greater role in the development of purity-impurity opposition. Dumont states that the author of the Laws of Manu, and the Jatakas show that there was a very strong feeling of impurity among certain groups and that of untouchables.[36] Dutt who is exponent for religious scripts, has taken into account 'a principle of ceremonial purity and touch-me- notism'.[37] Sharma, too, discerns the origin of untouchability in the combined ideas of taboo and impurity.[38] One can infer that a belief in Shastras contributed to the development of the notion of untouchability.

Contact and Untouchability

The notion of untouchability is not only confined to scripts but it is spread among the groups of Hindus and other neighbour groups like Muslim[39] also. Thus, the wide-spread practice became a matter of institution of untouchability. Dumont refers Stevenson's explanation of forms of contact 'attached to marriage and to food and drink'.[40] Notions of pollution through physical contacts are developed not only against the persons belonging to the impure castes, but also the contacts of those persons to the objects such as vessels and utensils, courtyard of a temple, a siting floor, an interior of a house, a place of locality or a residence, a food and the like. While interacting, rules of prohibitions and restrictions are observed against each caste of the community in a more or less form of avoidance or acceptance. The *notion has functional dimension in regulating interactional relations of commensality and intermarriage.*

Professor R.S. Sharma refers the scriptural injunctions regarding commensality.[41] What is stated in the ancient Shastras, is passed down till today. The notion of untouchability is so deeply imbibed that once the stigma is attributed to one's caste remains for a long time. For example, none of the Khalapur Chamars have engaged in their previous leather jobs for more than a century[42] but the stigma is still continued. The impact of *'ideas of taboo and impurity'* is manifested not only in villages, but also in towns and cities, however, a lesser. It can be illustrated through some of the incidents recently reported in newspapers and periodicals. Incidents: (1) Caste Hindu woman of Jamnagar city in Gujarat preferred to die rather than to get operated by the ex-untouchable surgeon.[43] (2) A statue of Dr. Sampurnananda, a master of sanskrit was to be unveiled on Jan. 24,1978 at Varanasi city by Jagjivan Ram, a senior minister in the Central Cabinet. While going to unveil, meanwhile, the students of the University opened the covered cloth over the statue and declared amongst themselves unveiled. However, as it was proposed, Jagjivan Ram unveiled it formally. But very soon the students of the University purified it with the water of Ganga (river) assuming that the statue was polluted by the touch of an ex-untouchable minister.[44] (3) Mr. Yogendra Makwana (ex-untouchable), a State Minister for Agriculture in the Central Cabinet uttered in a public meeting in Delhi that he was never allowed to enter the temple by the priests.[45] (4) Mr. Kasture (ex-untouchable), a Cabinet Minister in the State of

Maharashtra, was prevented from entering Balaji temple by the priest at Mehekar town, district Buldhana in Maharashtra.[46] (5) A tradition of the rite of placing a vessel (Ghatsthapana) by a local tahsildar (revenue officer of a taluka) became prevalent in Ambad municipal town (a taluka in Aurangabad district of Maharashtra). Tahsildar, Mr Suryavanshi was a Chamar by caste, an ex-untouchable. In order to avoid him from performing the rites, he was transferred elsewhere under the leadership of Municipal President, Mr.Bhalchandra Kulkarni with the help of local Assistant Tahsildar and the district Collector of Aurangabad (Maharashtra).[47]

The above few examples of reported incidents are sufficient to reveal the evidence of purity-impurity opposition. The above incidents reveal the experiences of Ministers and government Gazetted officers relating their caste disabilities observed in public places. On the basis of such experiences one can imagine the worst of common ex-untouchables. Through such recent examples one can perceive that how the notion of untouchability is deeply rooted even in the present changing circumstances.

Untouchability and Immobility

From the above discussion it is clear that there is interplay between untouchability and immobility. Taking into account the established order of the older view, Bernard Barber stated that 'social mobility is both impossible and immoral in this worldly life'.[48] Considering time dimension, Srinivas states: 'Pre-British Indian society was stationary in character, it did not preclude the mobility, upward as well as downward of individual castes in local hierarchy'.[49] In the context of association between caste and occupation, and contemptuous occupations and untouchability notion, the study of Saberwal (1973) confirms the foregoing discussion. On the basis of Modelpur town (in Punjab[50]) study, Saberwal revealed that certain pollution levels regarded with hereditary occupation of caste, and the pollution notion shifted from ancestral to occupational.[51] So in traditional India the practice of untouchability is nothing but the prevention from the upper-status giving occupations and also the interactional relationships with the upper caste-Hindus.

II

SOCIAL MOBILITY

Dr. B.R. Ambedkar, the champion of ex-untouchables, who had described the social condition of disabilities of untouchables in 1919[52] was a reality. The immobility character of Indian society is no more longer. Recent various developments such as; growth of modern education and industries, adoption of democratic and secular values, development of egalitarian laws and compensatory discrimination[53] through legislations are the modern factors giving way to mobility towards the adoption of modern occupations and to develop social intercourse. These developments encouraged the members of scheduled caste groups recently to abandon their caste occupation and adopt modern ones. The entry of scheduled caste persons into the modern occupations consequently appears to be useful for new and wider interactions along with the upper caste-Hindus. Since some decades the State has sanctioned the 'open norm system'[54] and it is gradually replacing the 'closed norm system'.[55] That is why, during the recent times the ex-untouchables can find their place in modern occupations and consequently in social mobility as well.

As discussed above, the hereditary nature of occupation and the established notion of untouchability are seen as factors for occupational and as well social immobility of ex-untouchables. In recent times, with the growth of industries and technological developments and also, the modern administrative and market systems the multitude of occupations came into existence. In such circumstances the nature of occupation cannot remain hereditary one. In consequence, the number of occupational opportunities are created. In this context, three questions arise. First, whether ex-untouchables are allowed to choose any occupation? Second, if allowed, are they capable to adopt it? Third, whether occupational role would find them useful to attain social mobility? These questions are so pertinent because the present Indian society is in such a phase of transition. Another fact is that the ex-untouchables do not have a background of knowledge of modern occupation. Also one has to come across with the difficulty of financial support to start an occupation as a source of self-employment. Even if one possesses knowledge of an occupation and the money to invest, again one has to face with the requirement of an accommodation to start it. Accommodation is not easy to him to get from an upper caste-Hindu owner.[56] In such a background, some additional questions arise. First, what determines occupational mobility of an Individual? If occupational mobility takes place, does it contribute to upward social mobility? If so, what factors contribute to social mobility? To answer all these questions, it needs some conceptual and theoretical discussion of occupational and social mobility.

Function of Occupation

Occupation has been the most common indicator of stratification.[57] It determines social position of individual, style of life and opportunities of life chances through income and the prestige of occupation. Considering prestige rank of occupations, the lowest status of the ex-untouchables can be accounted for their traditional occupations in the caste hierarchy. In contrast, an adoption of modern and other upper caste-Hindus' traditional occupations such as carpentry, tailoring, clothes-washing, and the like accounts for the higher status in the hierarchy. If social status is the function of occupation, then, by adopting modern occupation the status of SC person must be raised in the system of a stratification. It is not only limited to the particular person alone but also it contributes to other members of the person's family and consequently to the group to which one belongs. Thus occupational mobility can be instrumental to social mobility.

Social Mobility

Generally, social mobility is conceived as the transition from one social stratum to another. Sorokin conceives it "as change in status".[58] He classified mobility into horizontal and vertical. Our concern is vertical mobility, which meant 'the relations of an individual from one social stratum to another'.[59] To Tumin, social mobility is thought of 'opportunity of movement from one position to another in society'.[60] The Dictionary of Sociology refers social mobility as 'the movement of individuals between different levels of social hierarchy in occupational matters'[61] which is our focus.

In the light of the above meaning of social mobility, it has dimension of a social sanction. With regard to the meaning of 'Dictionary of Sociology', it has occupational dimension. Both social and occupational dimensions can be considered for discussion. Social in the sense, whether the norms of the society approve social mobility. And occupational in sense, whether the norms of the society allow for occupational mobility. In fact, social mobility has no meaning without the consideration of occupational mobility. In absence of occupational mobility, the conception of social mobility is futile. Because, *occupational mobility is the prime source of social mobility.* In the present study occupational mobility is considered as an independent variable to measure social mobility. It is for the reason that in traditional Hindu society, neither social mobility nor occupational mobility has a sanction. If the ex-untouchables are after attaining social mobility through occupational mobility, the old normative pattern of sanction has to be flexible. When scheduled caste persons in post-Independent India are found to be adopted modern occupations, it means that some noticeable changes must have been brought about in the established normative patterns of traditional India. Thus, in the light of ex-untouchables' mobility, what new norms are presumed to be contributed to their mobility, is the point of discussion.

Barber discussed institutional norms for affecting social mobility in a society.[62] He discussed that in a closed system of caste, social mobility has been inaccessible to ex-untouchables in India and to Negroes in the U.S.. In spite of the recent developments of open norm system in the U.S. and the U.K., Lieberson and Fuguilt (1967)[63] and Krausz (1972)[64] have held that racial discrimination against non-Whites has limited thè opportunities in modern occupational structure. Further, Barber discussed multiple elements towards the factors which produce mobility. In support of his statement he has mentioned interconnected factors of social mobility such as in the United States an ambitious family, a good education, and an expanding socio-economic system, and in a modern Dutch city as Heek listed out three ethnological, six socio-psychological and sociological, and four socio-economical.[65] Yamaguchi pointed out money and other tangible assets, knowledge and skill, social networks, race, sex, and education as resources for occupational attainment.[66]

Though Barber stood for multiple factors, he referred single factor analysis in some cases. He revealed family background as crucial factor for social mobility in all societies. For evidence, he quoted

Moulin's study of Nobel Prize winners, 1952 study of Warner and Abegglen on 'Occupational Mobility in American Business and Industry', Miller's study of the U.S. top business leaders, and Keller's study showing a similar trend of 'class inheritance pattern and mobility'.[67] He discussed wealth background to maintain the class position and further advancement also.[68] While discussing educational background, it is illustrated through the findings of Mulligan's study and in case of Russian Government's favour by providing educational facilities to the students of proletarian origin revealed that; the students of *better parental background* received *better advantage of education.*[69] In fact, none of the background of family, wealth or education is available to those of ex-untouchable persons. So, mobility of ex-untouchables requires to be discussed in the light of the development of a *new social system.* In a closed system of caste, mobility of ex-untouchables was not visible and now it is visible, it means some changes are occured in the old system with the introduction of new institutionalised pattern of open system.

Development of New Social System

The concept of social system refers to a process of interaction, normatively and motivationally oriented to a situation of social, physical and cultural objects.[70] Taking into account the aspects of this definition, the development of new social system in present India can be discussed. Legal normative pattern in present India has influenced the traditional customary pattern. Many welfare measures encouraged the occupational aspirations of the ex-untouchables in a situation of growing industrialization and changing criteria of social status. Hindus are no longer committed to their old order of Dharma. Hence, their cultural or religious values are changing according to the Constitutional framework. The background of socio-cultural movements, anti-disabilities legislation, patterns of urban setting, growth of modern industrial and administrative system, role of motivational aspect, educational and occupational achievements have been found to be contributed to the new social system. These factors, in general, can be considered and discussed towards the sources of mobility.

Socio-Cultural Movements

Professor K.L. Sharma indicated 'socio-cultural movement' as a factor affecting social mobility among the Scheduled Caste.[71] Maharashtra is known as the land of movements.[72] The spirit of movements was reformatory in character. The movements were found useful in bringing about changes in the institutions of religion, caste and marriage. First, especially in the background of Kolhapur, the social movement engineered by Shahu Chhatrapati[73] was rebellious in its character. In fact, he launched a campaign against the order of the 'Brahman Dharma'. He brought about many reformatory and revolutionary changes in social, religious, educational, occupational, and other fields of life. His actions influenced the way of life of people in Kolhapur region, in general, and in particular, it encouraged the ex-untouchable people to come forward with confidence and self-respect. Second, the movement led by Dr. Babasaheb Ambedkar[74] deeply rooted especially among the Mahars, the largest section of ex-untouchable castes. The movement of ex-untouchables concentrated on the possession of a political power, a struggle for civil right, an educational achievement, and reservations in services. Recently, the government adopted the policy of encouraging self-employment. Studies of Gare-Limaye (1970),[75] Patwardhan (1973),[76] Kulkarni-Hiramani (1975)[77] and Rahate (1985),[78] have reported the impact of movements led by Dr. Babasaheb Ambedkar which brought about social and occupational changes among the neo-Buddhists (former Mahars).

Compensatory Discrimination and Anti-disabilities Legislation

Chekki has taken into account the facts of law for social mobility.[79] Compensatory discrimination means by which educational, political, and economic interests of the Scheduled Caste members are safeguarded by special Constitutional and other Statutory provisions.[80] The policy of compensatory discrimination was introduced by the British India Government and after independence it is continued and extended to wider benefits especially for Scheduled Castes and Scheduled Tribes. The measures adopted for the upliftment of Scheduled Castes are relating to educational, professional, political and economic in type. Educational facilities are provided in the form of scholarship, hostel accommodation, and reservation in admissions for career courses. Facilities of reservation are provided for jobs and promotions in government and other sectors. There is a provision of reservation in political bodies from village panchayat to parliament and in other corporate bodies of the government. During the recent period financial benefits such as loans, special grants, subsidies and other concessions are extended to the deprived sections of the community. Therefore, K.L. Sharma pointed out that; 'the welfare measures have induced a certain level of mobility among the Scheduled Caste'.[81]

Untouchability is abolished by Art.17 of the Constitution of India. In order to oblige the Art. 17, the Government of India passed Untouchability Offence Act of 1955 (now it is entitled as the Protection of Civil Rights Act) to remove social disabilities of the ex-untouchables. Constitution guarantees freedom of occupation and any prevention from choosing other occupation or forcing to carry out the polluting or menial tasks is forbidden and made penal by law.[82] Marc Galanter (1972) generalized some of the impact of anti-disabilities legislation such as; ex-untouchables' unimaginable participation in public life, entry into political and administrative power positions of the government and increasing number of higher educated persons.[83] Further, he observes decline of disabilities comparatively 'more in urban than in rural areas,... more in public and occupational life than in social and family matters; ...more among the educated than among the uneducated; more among men than among women'.[84] Moreover, he identified the impact in the form of 'promoting new patterns of behaviour, direct effect as an instrument for the prosecution of offenders, as an educational device, and to believe that untouchability is gone or going'.[85] In fact, it is not easy to measure the direct impact of legislation at socio-psychological level. But, what can be the influence of legislation can be judged from the argument forwarded by Jagjivan Ram[86] that: 'If a chamar's son becomes a sub-inspector a Brahmin constable will salute him. Imagine what kind of social revolution it is when a bhangi's son becomes a district magistrate?'[87] Thus, institutionalization of post-Independent compensatory legislation is shaking up the customary laws.

Patterns of Urban Setting

In the context of Kolhapur city as the unit of present study, the patterns of urban setting are accounted for the discussion. It has many aspects in contrast to the rural setting in India. In rural India, ex-untouchables cannot fight and if they fight fail to get justice against the rule of caste order and the tyranny of caste Hindu landlords. Because, ex-untouchables are poor in muscle strength and wealth as well. They have to depend on caste-Hindu landlords for their daily bread. Formal police control also stands by caste-Hindus. Thus, government also fails to give protection to those of ex-untouchables from the local muscle power. In contrast to this rural background, urban setting is characterised by heterogeneous, contractual and impersonal relations, predominance of formal controls, and prevalence of secular norms. Such urban environment promotes individual freedom, secular attitude and anonymity. Moreover, it promotes for especially occupational and social mobility.

What Chekki (1971) observed is worth mentioning here, that: 'social stratification in modern urban India, though based on caste, is not closed, rigid and immobile but happens to be open flexible and mobile'.[88] Further he adds:'Industrialization and urbanization have tended to reduce social distance among different castes. A Brahman and a Scheduled Caste (the ex-untouchable) person work shoulder to shoulder in a modern factory or office, without any social inhibitions.'[89] That is why, many ex-untouchables migrate from their villages of birth-place. To them, cities have become the centres of their protest and agitational activities relating to social, economic, political, etc. Thus, city becomes a community of social mobility through occupational and other channels. It can be evidenced as Patwardhan (1973) indicated: "Urbanization and the urban situation constitute an important variable in bringing about social change and mobility, particularly for the former polluting castes".[90]

Development of Modern Administrative and Industrial Systems

Communications and crime prevention were regarded the duties of Mahars in traditional India. British India Government introduced separate departments of Post-office and Police service. Now in post-Independent India it is fully established. In modern India, these postal and police departments have completely withdrawn the traditional duties of the Mahars. Modern industries producing nylon ropes. Now electrical sound service became available at village level too. All it is being widely used by the people. Such better availability of modern goods and services withdrawn the traditional jobs of the Mangs of making ropes and drumming the leather sound- instruments. Availability of Kirloskar engine in the market withdrawn the services of the Chamars of providing leather bags to the farmers.

Modern tanning and leather industries made many Chamars and Dhors unemployed. Drainage and use of flush vessel system too reduced the services of Bhangis. All these developments of administrative and industrial systems gave way to occupational mobility and made them possible to be away from their filthy jobs. Consequently, it helped in reducing the pure-impure notion of caste-Hindus and making them ready for commensal and other interactions with ex-untouchable members.

Role of Motivational Factor

The persons from ex-untouchable castes suffer from a certain feeling of diffidence about self-employed occupations.[91] Perhaps, it is because they possess neither experience nor traditional background of confidence of success for modern self-employed occupational career. In such a background, the role of motivational factor needs some discussion.

The term 'motivation' is employed in the study of psychology in its variety of forms. Different approaches are also developed to study the motivation of persons in society. Therefore, Atkinson, a leading psychologist who studied 'motivation', states: 'The term has no fixed technical meaning in contemporary psychology'.[92] He mentioned the early use in reference to "what causes". Despite its different meanings, Atkinson recommended 'determinants of direction, vigour, and persistence of action' towards a theory and a conception of motivation.[93] In this present study *what causes* or *determinants of direction* ..., can be applied towards its conception of motivation factor.

Crockett's analysis (1974) has shown the role of motivation that 'highly motivated men attained occupations higher in the status hierarchy than those of their fathers'.[94] It supports that occupational mobility has motivational dimension. Of course, there is no doubt about the role of motivational factor which influences the occupational mobility among ex-untouchables.

O'Malley long back (1932) noted a psychological factor as one of the reasons for the abandonment of hereditary occupations. He observed: "the ambition of the low castes to raise themselves in social esteem by adopting some pursuit which by common repute is more respectable than their ancestral calling".[95] Further, he elaborated: 'Social ambition of this kind is laudable enough: it is based on a certain sense of self-respect'.[96] Now, to come back to "what causes" or "determinants of direction ...", when occupational mobility is observed comparatively more among the Mahars, it has a history of Dr. Ambedkar's 'movement' of self-respect,[97] and a background of development of modern administration and industries, developments in modern legislative norms and secular patterns of urban environment to construe for motivational factor.

Educational and Occupational Attainment

It is not sufficient to have merely the development of new modern social systems but as a result of it, some educational and occupational entry requires to be visible empirically among the scheduled castes. In a modern society without educational attainment i.e., academically higher or vocationally skilled, progressive change is difficult to understand. The progress of scheduled castes can be measured by their educational growth and occupational deviation from caste to modern. In the context of present study, Maharashtra is selected for the review of scheduled castes' progress in education and modern occupations.

According to 1981 Census, the literacy percentage among the total population of SCs in Maharashtra is 35.55,[98] whereas according to 1961 Census it was 15.78.[99] It indicates for their general educational growth. According to a reported study of 1972, '60 per cent of the post-matric scholarships went to the three States viz., Maharashtra, West Bengal, and Uttar Pradesh, though these states have only 39 per cent of the total Scheduled Castes population in the country. Within Maharashtra, 78 per cent of the scholarships were claimed by the Mahar community which constitutes 35 per cent of the Scheduled Castes population in the State.'[100] It further indicates that scheduled castes in Maharashtra are ahead in receiving higher education. Suma Chitnis reported that among 2,97,386 total number of students enrolled for all Degree courses in Maharashtra, 21,271 students were enrolled from scheduled castes.[101] Further, she pointed out, that the representation of the scheduled castes in the prestigious professional courses (Medicine, Engineering and Technology) was better than their representation in the less prestigious professional courses (Commerce and Law).[102] It again indicates for specific development towards the professional courses. This educational growth accompanied with governmental measures accrues for representation in service occupations. This continuing growth in educational attainment of scheduled castes suggests for their increasing representation in service categories of Class IV to Class I in the different Departments of the State and the Central Government. For example, a representation of SC in State and Central Government services for Maharashtra which was 2.10 percentage in Class I category on dt. 1.1.1971,[103] increased to 6.28 percentage in the same category on dt. 1.1.1979.[104] About the representation in other occupations, specific figures are not available for representation of SCs in self-employed categories of modern occupations such as medicine, engineering, business, trade, advocacy in the Courts, etc. But, their rising entry in non-polluting and prestigious occupations is visible.

Generally, it is observed that the persons from ex-untouchable category who are engaged in white-collar or modern jobs are seen acceptable to the upper caste-Hindus for commensal interactions. Gangrade (1975) reported that such attainments found helpful to Chamars of village Chhattera in Haryana for commensality.[105] Thus, the development of new social system can be construed as one side of the coin and the attainments by scheduled castes as the other for the outcome of social mobility.

To sum up, the traditional order of Dharma regarded contemptuous occupations as impure. As the ex-untouchables have been engaged in such occupations so are prohibited for interactional relations with the upper caste-Hindus. But the post-Independent democratic laws and special legislations in the interests of the scheduled castes, and also a growing modern industrialization gave way to the new patterns of social system. Under such modern setting occupational and social mobility of the ex-untouchables needs to be examined.

Now, let us see what the previous studies on occupational mobility have revealed to the varied attributes.

NOTES AND REFERENCES

1. Ibbetson, Denzil Charles Jelf: 'Punjab Castes'; Philadelphia, U.S.A., 1916, p. 2.
2. Karve, Irawati: What is Caste? Caste and Occupation, *The Economic Weekly*, Vol. X, No. 12, 1958, pp. 401-407.
3. Ghurye, G.S.: *Caste and Race in India,* Popular Prakashan, Bombay, 1969, p. 15.
4. Ibid., pp. 15-16.
5. Buhler, G.: *The Laws of Manu*; trans., Motilal Banarasidass, Delhi (Reprint), 1975, p. 24.

6. Ibid., p. 423.
7. Ibid., p. 430.
8. According to Manu 'the King has been created (to be) the protector of castes (Varna) and orders, who all according to their rank, discharge their several duties' (See Buhler, G.: *op. cit.*, p. 221).
9. Prof. N.G. Bhavare quoted Shivaji's letter of Jan. 28, 1677 (trans.) in B.R. Kamble's (ed.) *'Studies in Shivaji and His times'*; Shivaji University Publication, Kolhapur, 1982, p. 188.
10. See, Govt. of Maharashtra: Dr. *Babasaheb Ambedkar Writings and Speeches,* Vol. I, 1979, p. 274.
11. Bopegamage, A.: Caste and Poverty in *Sociology and Social Research*, Vol. 57, October, 1972, p. 66.
12. Ibid., p. 68.
13. Incidence reported in *Maharashtra Times* (Marathi daily), dt. 1.2.1966. Collected by N.D. Kamble for his 'Atrocities on Scheduled Castes in Post-Independent India'; Institute of Social and Economic Change, Bangalore (Typescript), p. 54.
14. N.D. Kamble; *Ibid,* p. 67.
15. *Ibid,* p. 71.
16. *Ibid,* p. 86.
17. *Ibid,* p. 157.
18. *Ibid,* p. 203.
19 Buddhists of today in Maharashtra are identified by caste Mahar, an ex-untouchable caste.
20. Manohar (*Marathi Weekly*), Pune, Oct. 22-28, 1978, p. 27.
21. Kulkarni, M.G.: 'The Scheduled Castes in Maharashtra: A Study in Social Change with Particular Reference to Mahars (Buddhists)', *Marathwada University Journal,* Vol. IX, July, 1969.
22. Mahar, J.M. (Ed.): 'The Untouchables in Contemporary India', Arizona Press, Tucson, Arizona, 1972, pp. 29-30.
23. According to Vishnu, "in times of distress, each caste may follow the occupation of that next (below) to it in rank" (II.15)... a Brahman in distress might with little discredit take to the fighting and ruling professions of the Kshatriyas, and more blemish would attach to the following of agriculture, trade and other professions of Vaisyas. Baudhayana, too, allows the profession of a warrior to a Brahman who cannot support himself by his own professions (II.2.4.16). According to Gautama, "agriculture and trade are also lawful for a Brahman provided he does not do the work himself; likewise lending money at interest" (X.5.6), ... "In times of distress of Kshatriya may follow the occupations of a Vaisya" (Gautama VII.26) ... from Kautilya's Arthasastra that: "the Kshatriyas of Kamboja, Saurastra and other countries live by agriculture, trade and profession of arms" (BK.XI. Ch.I). This version cited from: N.K. Dutt's *Origin and Growth of Caste in India,* Vol. I, Mukhopadhyaya, 1968, pp. 121-122.
24 The injunctions laid down by Manu are mentioned below:
    (i) 'A Brahman may accept (gifts) from anybody; for according to the law it is not possible (to assert) that anything pure can be sullied [Manu X. 102] (Buhler, G.: *op. cit.,* p. 424).
    (ii) 'By teaching, by sacrificing for, and by accepting gifts from despicable (men) Brahmanas (in distress) commit not sin; for they (are as pure) as fire and water' [Manu X. 103] (Buhler, G.: *op. cit.*).
    (iii) 'A Brahmana who is unable to maintain himself, should (rather) glean ears or grains from (the field of) any (man); gleaning ears is

better than accepting gifts, picking up single grains is declared to be still more laudable'. [Manu X. 112] (Buhler, G.: *op. cit.,* p. 425).

(iv) 'A Vaisya who is unable to subsist by his own duties, may even maintain himself by a Sudra's mode of life, avoiding (however) acts forbidden (to him), and he should give it up, when he is able (to do so)'. [Manu X. 98] (Buhler, G.: *op. cit.,* p. 423).

25. Sharma, R.S.: *Sudras in Ancient India*, Motilal Banarasidass, Delhi, 1958, pp. 123-124.
26. Thaper, Romila: Art., 'Social Mobility in Ancient India', in *Indian Society: Historical Probings*, (ed.), PPH, 1974, p. 108.
27. Dumont, Louis: *Homo Hierarchicus*, Vikas Publications, 1970, p. 93.
28. Ibid.
29. Ibid., p. 44.
30. Ibid.
31. Ibid.
32. Ibid., p. 54.
33. Ibbetson, Denzil Charles Jelf: *op. cit.,* pp. 5-6.
34. Ghurye, G.S.: *op. cit.,* p. 214.
35. Dumont, Louis: *op. cit.,* p. 59.
36. Ibid., p. 53.
37. Dutt, N.K.: *Origin and Growth of Caste in India,* Vol. I, Mukhopadhyaya, 1968, p. 111.

Dutt elaborated further:

"During the Brahmana period we come across for the first time mentions of ceremonial purity and impurity attaching to certain persons or castes on sacrificial grounds. So the Sudra was not to touch the milk at the specially sacred fire sacrifice (Tait. Br. III. 2.3.). He was not to be treated as a member of the sacrificing community on sacrificial grounds and with him there should be no free intercourse on the sacred spot by men engaged in secret ceremonies (S.P. Br. III.1.1.). Thus tne touch of a carpenter was regarded as impure during the celebration of sacrificial rites, which had to be removed by the sprinkling of sacrificial water (S.P. Br. I.1.3.12.). So far as the Sudras and artisans were concerned, the idea of defilement by touch was confined within the enclosure of the sacrificial ground and did not extend to ordinary circumstances of life. Eventually the two ideas, the idea of ceremonial purity on sacrificial grounds, and the idea of defilement by the touch of a very unclean, repulsive being, invaded the position of the Sudras and those reduced to their rank from two sides until their touch came to be regarded as impure not only at sacrificial rites but on all occasions of life, especially in the matter of food and drink (pp. 111-112).

38 To Quote:

"Against the background of a very material culture of the aborigins, the increasing contempt of manual work, combined with primitive ideas of taboo and impurity associated with certain materials, produced the unique social phenomenon of untouchability. This was particularly true of the work of 'candalas who dealt with corpses, with which were linked primitive ideas of impurity and horror. Consequently it was felt necessary to avoid contact with such persons. In later times the idea of untouchability was extended not only to the nisadas and pulkusas but also to craftsmen such as the leather workers and weavers' (See Sharma, R.S.: *Sudras in Ancient India*, Motilal Banarasidass, Delhi, 1958, pp. 132-133).

39 For example, Muslims of Village Kanpur Kasba of Etawah district do not allow 'Bhangis' (scavengers) to touch their well (*Indian Express*, Bombay, May 18, 1984, quoted in article by Nirmala Srinivasan).

40. Dumont, Louis: *op. cit.*, p. 131.

41 'The texts of the period repeatedly state that a Brahmana should not accept the food of a Sudra, for it reduces his spiritual strength (Asvamedhi Ka Parvan, (SE) 110.17-20, 61.44.45; Brahaspati, Sraddha Khanda, verse 43.7. The Santi Parvan does not allow the Brahmana to take the food of Carpenters, leather workers, washermen and dyers. According to Yajnavalkya the food of the Sudras and outcastes (Patitas) is not permitted to a Snataka. He further specifies that a Snataka should not take the food of a stage-player, a bamboo worker, a goldsmith, a weapon seller, an artisan, a tailor, a dyer, one whose living is by dogs, a butcher, a washerman or an oilmaker. The Anusasana Parvan declares that the man who takes food from a Sudra swallows the very abomination of the earth, drinks the excretions of the human body, and partakes of the filth of all the world' (See; Sharma, R.S.: Ibid, 1958, p. 256).

42. Mahar, J.M. (ed.): *The Untouchables in Contemporary India*, Arizona, Tucson, Arizona, 1972, pp. 23-24.

43. *The Times of India*, Bombay, dated 7.11.1971.

44. *Dharmayug* (Hindi Weekly), *The Times of India* Publication, Bombay, April 30 to May 6, 1978. In another occasion, Jagjivan Ram reveals his experience: 'Even I am not a touchable. Will a Brahmin call me to his house for a meal? May be Mrs. Gandhi would have done so (*India Today,* April 15, 1985, p. 61).

45. *Bahujan Nayak* (Marathi Weekly), Nagpur, dt. 22.4.1984.

46. N.D. Kamble; *op. cit.*, p. 204.

47. *Purogami Satyashodhak* (Marathi Quarterly), Pune, dated 4.12.1977.

48. Barber, Bernard: Art., 'Social Mobility in Hindu India' in James Silverberg (ed.): *Social Mobility in the Caste System in India*, 1968, p. 19.

49. Srinivas, M.N.: Art., "Mobility in the Caste System' in Singer and Cohn (ed.): Structure and Change in Indian Society; Aldine, 1968, p. 189.
Bailey also reported untouchability as an obstacle to mobility (See; Bailey, F.G.: Caste and Economic frontier; Manchester University Press, 1957, p. 275).

50 Punjab is reported for its lesser observance of purity-impurity opposition if compared to other parts of India. Because, Sikhism does not preach discrimination. But in Punjab, Hindus also live together with Sikhs. Yet the study suggests the prevalence of untouchability-notion associated with the occupations of ex-untouchables.

51. Saberwal, S.: 'Receding Pollution: Intercaste Relations in Urban Punjab', *Sociological Bulletin,* Vol. 22, 1973, p. 254.

52 'The very untouchability attached to their person is a bar to their moral and material progress. The principal modes of acquiring wealth are trade, industry or service. The untouchables can engage in none of these because of their untouchability. From an untouchable trader no Hindu will buy' (Dr. B.R. Ambedkar had described in a statement submitted to Southborough Committee. See; Dr. Babasaheb Ambedkar: Writings and Speeches; Vol. I; The Education Department, Government of Maharashtra, Bombay, 1979, p. 261).

53 The term preferred and used by Marc Galanter for 'protective discrimination' policies of Government of India in the interest of Scheduled Castes and Scheduled Tribes (Galanter, Marc: Competing Equalities, Oxford, 1984, p. 2).

54 Open norm system based on legality and rationality.

55 Closed norm system based on ascribed status.

56 Incident of Surat city (Gujarat) is reported that caste Hindus refused to give shops in market area (See; Parmar, Y.A.: Art. 'Occupational Variation in a Scheduled Caste of Surat—A Case of Mahayavanshi', *South Gujarat University Journal*, Vol. X, 1981, p. 12). When I was at Latur (district in Maharashtra), I was told that a Gujarat owner of plots refused to sell a plot to Mr. Katake, an ex-untouchable, who was to use it for scrap-iron shop.

57. Lipset and Zetleberg: 'A Theory of Social Mobility' in Bendix and Lipset (ed.) *Class, Status and Power*, Free Press, 1966, p. 562.

58. Sorokin, P.A.: *Social and Cultural Mobility*, Free Press, 1964, p. 11.

59. Ibid., p. 133.

60. Tumin, Melvin M.: *Social Stratification*, Prentice-Hall, India, New Delhi, 1981 (EEE), p. 87.

61. Abercrombie, Nicholas; Hill, Stephen and Turner, Bryan S.: *Dictionary of Sociology;* Penguin, 1984, p. 196.

62. Barber, Bernard: *Social Stratification*; Harcourt Brace and World, 1957, p. 456.

63. Lieberson, S. and Fuguilt, G.V.: 'Negro-White Occupational Differences in the Absence of Discrimination' *American Journal of Sociology*, Vol. 74, No. 2, Sept. 1967, p. 197.

64. Krausz, Ernest: 'Factors of Social Mobility in British Minority Groups'; *The British Journal of Sociology*, Vol. 23, 1972, p. 276.

65. Barber, Bernard: *op. cit.*, 1957, pp. 357-8.

66. Yamaguchi, Kazuo: 'The Structure of Intergenerational Occupational Mobility: Generality and Specificity in Resources, Channels, and Barriers'; *American Journal of Sociology*, Jan. 1983, Vol. 88, No. 4.

67. Barber, Bernard: *op. cit.*, pp. 456 and 459.

68. Ibid., pp. 375-389.

69. Ibid., pp. 399-403.

70. Parsons did not define 'social system' in a sentence or two but treated it a process and so constructed it. For detail definition of concept, see; Parsons, Talcott: *The Social System*, Routledge and Kegan Paul Ltd., London, 1970, Chap. 1.

71. Sharma, K.L.: 'Caste and Class: Factors Affecting Social Mobility Among the Scheduled Castes', *The Journal of Sociological Studies*, Vol. 2, Jan. 1983, p. 55.

72 Movements led in Maharashtra: Mahatma Jotiba Phule's 'Satya Shodhak' (truth-finder), Swami Dayanand's 'Arya Samaj' for social equality emphasizing inter-caste marriages, Kolhapur's Rajarshi Shahu Chhatrapati's socio-educational, Maharshi Vitthal Ramji Shinde's 'Depressed Class Mission' for education, Karmaveer Bhaurao Patil's "Rayat Education Society' for education especially to ruralites, Dr. Babasaheb Ambedkar's socio-cultural-educational, at present Dr. Baba Adhav's socio-cultural, and the like.

73 Please see; Appendix II: 'Role of the Reformers'.

74 Please see; Appendix II: 'Role of the Reformers'.

75. Gare, Govind and Limaye, Shirubhau: Maharashtratil Dalit - Shodh aani Bodh (Marathi), Sahaddhyayan Prakashan, Bombay, 1970.

76. Patwardhan, Sunanda: *Change Among India's Harijans*, Orient Longman, 1973.

77. Kulkarni, M.G. and Hiramani, A.B.: 'Occupational Pattern in two Marathwada villages - a comparative study, *Marathwada University Journal*, Vol. XIV, No. 2, September, 1975.

78. Rahate, J.V.: 'Modernization Among Scheduled Castes With Special Reference to Mahars, Weavers and Sweepers of Nagpur City' (Marathi); Ph.D. dissertation (unpublished), 1985.

79. Chekki, D.A.: 'Social Stratification and Trends of Social Mobility in Modern India', *The Indian Journal of Social Work*, Vol. 31, No. 4, Jan. 1971, p. 379.
80 Please see: Appendix: 'Relevant Articles from the Constitution of India'.
81. Sharma, K.L.: *op. cit.*, p. 55.
82. Provision 7-A of Untouchability Offence Act, 1955 states: Whoever compels any person, on the ground of 'untouchability' to do any scavenging or sweeping or to remove any caracass or to flay any animal or to remove the umbilical cord or do any other job of a similar nature, shall be deemed to have enforced a disability arising out of 'untouchability'.
83. Galanter, Marc: 'The Abolition of Disabilities—Untouchability and the Laws'; See; Mahar, J. Michael (ed.): *The Untouchables in Contemporary India*, Arizona Press, Tucson, Arizona, 1972, p. 261.
84. Ibid., p. 262.
85. Ibid.
86 Who enjoyed most of his political career being senior minister in the Central Cabinet.
87. See; *India Today*, April 15, 1985, p. 61.
88. Chekki, D.A.: *op. cit.;* p. 378.
89. Ibid., p. 379.
90. Patwardhan, Sunanda: *op. cit.*, pp. 23 and 72.
91 To refer an example of technical degree holders from Scheduled Castes, that: A State Government sponsored Seminar was held in Tamil Nadu in which technically trained young persons belonging to Scheduled Castes were invited for career guidance so that the Scheduled Caste technicians would come forward to start with small industries of their own. It is reported from the discussion with Scheduled Caste degree holders that: in spite of all governmental assurances it found that they lack confidence to use their technical knowledge to start own industries and tendency to have preference towards the secured job in government department. See; *Kurukshetra*, New Delhi, April 16, 1977, p. 8.
92. Atkinson, J.W.: *An Introduction to Motivation*, Van Nostrand, 1964, p. 273.
93. Ibid., p. 274.
94. See; Atkinson, J.W. and Raynor, J.O.: *Motivation and Achievement,* Winston-Wiley, 1974, p. 27.
95. O' Malley, L.S.S.: *Indian Caste Customs*, Vikas, 1932, p. 126.
96. Ibid., p. 127.
97 For movement led by Dr. Ambedkar, please see: Appendix II: Role of the Reformers.
98. *Census of India 1981*, Series-I, Part B(ii), Primary Census Abstract for Scheduled Castes; Registrar General and Census Commissioner, India, p. xxvii.
99. *Census of India 1961*, Vol. X - Maharashtra, Part V-A; Scheduled Castes and Scheduled Tribes in Maharashtra - Tables, Manager of Publications, Delhi-8, p. 36.
100. See; *Economic Times,* 15.12, 1980.
101. Chitnis, Suma: Literacy and Educational Enrolment Among the Scheduled Castes of Maharashtra, Tata Institute of Social Sciences, Bombay-88, 1974, p. 93.
102. Ibid., p. 94.
103. Adapted from Gaval, R.S.: *The Scheduled Castes and the Scheduled Tribes and their Service Privileges; Publisher*: Kumbhare, General Secretary, Republican Party of India, Diksha Bhoomi, Nagpur-10, 1974, See; Appendix 'D'

104. Report of the Commission for Scheduled Castes and Scheduled Tribes (July 1978-March 1979), Controller of Publication, Delhi-110054, 1980, Annexure-I, p. 163.
105. Gangrade, K.D.: "Social Mobility in India: a study of depressed class'; *Man in India*, Vol. 55, 3 Sept. 1975, p. 264.

TWO

Review of Previous Studies on Occupational Mobility

In this chapter, I have taken a review of studies, surveys and volumes in literature on mobility. These previous studies throw light on the area of mobility and social change at the levels of world, national and regional. The trends of mobility reported at each level differ so far as factors, its patterns, its nature and its extent are concerned.

Studies at the World Level

The studies referred here have dealt with the factors like structural determinants, and motivational aspects such as modern industrial developments, an educational attainment, and a background of family and religion, etc. These are discussed below.

Structural Determinants and Mobility Chances

Like groups of ex-untouchable castes in India, there are other groups elsewhere in the U.S., the U.K. and other European countries against whom discriminatory attitudes are developed merely because of their belongingness to the particular category of groups. The members of such groups are facing the problems of mobility chances along with obstacles to occupational and social advancements. In a discussion of the factors of mobility, Krausz has stated: "'race' or 'colour' is being held to be the most important factor limiting the opportunities and achievements of individuals".[1] Further he mentioned what Rex observed; 'that the Jewish minority occupies a position outside the stratification system whilst coloured groups are beneath it'.[2] With the evidences of other studies he suggests, 'that the relative immobility of coloured groups has been largely due to discrimination on grounds of the special racial factor of colour'.[3] In case of Jews, it is reported that: 'In many parts of

Europe they were not allowed to own land, and even in industry and trade they were pushed into peripheral or new enterprises'.[4] On the other hand, in spite of widespread discrimination practised against Jews in the spheres of employment, services and other fields, it did not prevent their mobility.[5] Again it is significant to note that Krausz made a reference of Sheila Patterson's field study in which it is stated: 'When comparing entry to employment and the employment situation of coloured immigrants, Irish, Poles and other Europeans, she found that on the whole colour was less important a factor than socio-cultural and educational background, and the possession of skills, aptitudes, adaptability and a knowledge of English'.[6] Thus, it is evident that *race, class and creed remained as determinants of discriminatory relationships between social groups all over the world.* However, by possessing certain capabilities some have attained mobility despite their colour background.

Class Structure and Occupational Stability and Mobility

The findings of Goldthorpe and Llewellyn on intergenerational occupational mobility and stability and class structure are based on the data from the survey enquiry into occupational mobility in England and Wales undertaken in 1972 and 1974. It reported that; the extent of intergenerational occupational mobility in class structure reveals relatively low among the individuals of the low-class origin. And the *parents who hold command over resources both material and cultural succeeded in maintaining their Class-I and II positions.*[7]

In another study, some similar type of evidence is reported: 'A rather high degree of intergenerational mobility is observed within the working class in England and within the petty burgeoisie in France'.[8] But, Swedish observation reveals rather different pattern from England and France, that; 'in Sweden the sons of manual wage-workers, including agricultural workers, and also of lower-level white-collar employees have achieved upward mobility into service-class positions'.[9]

Through these studies, it can be generalized that the *parents who possess resources, can aspire* for their children's ambitions.

Race and Occupation

Negroes in the U.S. were brought as slaves and later after abolition of slavery were employed in manual and non-profitable jobs for centuries until recently. It is informed that racial dissimilarities in occupational structure declined with each succeeding generation, but at a rather slow rate.[10] Non-Whites are still occupationally *disadvantaged.* Despite the equality in formal educational attainment, they did not obtain the same jobs as Whites. Liberson and Fuguilt study (1967) reported that Negroes overrepresented in lower jobs and less chances to be employed as manager, proprietor, sales worker and the like.[11] It is clear that racial factor predominates the employment market.

Civil Rights Movement and Non-White Professionals

Ransford mentioned, that: 'As opportunities increased for blacks, some obtained better-paying, skilled, blue-collar and white-collar positions'.[12] On the basis of Lloyd Warner's study in 1941, Ransford reported that: 'Lower-class blacks were far more disadvantaged in socio-economic characteristics than lower-class whites' and also, it is mentioned, that; 'it became increasingly possible for some high-achieving blacks to have greater status in the society at large than lower-class whites'.[13] These changes are noticed as a result of protective legislation in the interests of Blacks. As a result, they are entering into the decision-making positions and also they are exercising their collective power.[14]

In the context of interactional situations, it is mentioned that, due to the *Civil Rights Movement*, a large number of *Blacks* were found to be *moving* into high prestigeous occupations such as business, law, medicine, government, and military. In another situation it is discussed that in a large hospital a black doctor who had received the same respect and prestige as a white doctor, might experience discrimination into an upper-class neighbourhood or join a select social club due to the unequal profile of ethnicity.[15] In another instance, statistics showed that a middle class among Blacks and Chicanos in the U.S. was coming up. *Black* and Chicano professionals were entering private practice such as medical, veterinary and legal services, but were *forced into a segregated market-place* with a smaller and poorer clientele from which to draw.[16] It reveals that Civil Rights

Movement and *protective legislation proved little help* in joining the upper professional market.

Family Background and Motivation for Occupational Career

Some studies reported motivational aspects of mobility. Evidences of non-caste societies suggest that in spite of the discrimination and other obstacles, mobility was observed among the Jews as a result of their persistence of achievement-motivation factor.[17] In 1964 report, Goode had put that, 'family elements in motivation play a substantial role in the education and training that eventually leads to social mobility'.[18] He stated the importance of family background, that: 'It is in the family setting that the individual's motivation to achieve is developed, as well as the social and intellectual skills that hinder or help him in the first step along that road'.[19] He analysed the nexus of family variable to achievement motivation and mobility.[20] To quote Kelley:

> 'A son born into a high status family acquires economic resources which he then invests in education, physical capital, and the like, while a son from a low status family gets fewer resources to invest and is consequently at a disadvantage'.[21]

His hypothesis in the context of inheritance of wealth and family status is significant to note, that: 'There is greater inheritance of status in less-developed capitalist societies, in agrarian societies where land is privately owned, and in societies where wealth and income are more unequally distributed'. It is proved by cross-cultural data and indicated a clear tendency for status-inheritance to be the greatest in less-developed capitalist societies and in societies where income is more unequally distributed.[22] Another data of under-developed society, for example; Haiti showed that between two generations of males the decrease in the percentage of persons engaged in agriculture was relatively small, i.e., from 96 percent to 86 percent.[23] Moreover, Treiman and Terrell have shown in the comparative study, that: '(i) there is less intergenerational occupational mobility in Britain than in the United States, (ii) that this difference is apparently due to the stronger direct effect of father's occupational status on son's occupational status in Britain, since (iii) the effect of father's occupation on son's education and that of son's education on son's occupation are about equally strong in the two countries'.[24]

Thus, *opportunities in life and career depend on favourable family background* as well as motivation. Those who have these, find it easier to raise in the social ladder and to move wherever they like.

Religion and Occupational Accomplishment

Using Weberian theory of role of Protestantism in the development of Capitalism, some researchers studied the differences in occupational achievement by religion. On the basis of the most of the previous studies, Jackson and others reported that Catholics tend to come from lower occupational origin than the Protestants.[25] The same study suggested similar results that Protestants were more likely than Catholics of the same occupational origin to enter professional and business occupations.[26] It indicates the influence of *Protestant* socialization leading towards the development of professional career.

Education and Occupational Mobility

Kerckhoff and others studied the outcome of sons' occupational attainment in Great Britain. The findings reflect educational attainment significantly for occupational outcomes.[27] Another study of Kelley indicates the correlation between education and occupation to be substantial in all societies but the lowest in Toro, somewhat higher in Panama, Argentina and the U.S. and very high elsewhere.[28] In the comparative study of social mobility and the process of status attainment in Britain and the United States, Treiman and Terrell have shown that, 'despite large difference in the educational systems, the role of educational attainment in occupational mobility is highly similar in the two countries'.[29] In this way, in Western societies *educational attainment* is found to be significant for occupational mobility.

Studies at the National Level

I could not find studies showing correlation between occupational mobility leading to social mobility among scheduled castes and that too in urban setting. Hence I have referred to all the studies, both from rural and urban setting, which I could obtain. The sociological and anthropological studies conducted by Indian researchers on occupational mobility reported occupational shifting from menial to manual activities,[30] from own caste's activities to other manual jobs,[31] from manual to skilled and government jobs, as well as jobs in private sectors[32] and from unclean to clean works.[33] Very few studies[34] reported "no change" in the traditional occupational pattern. Study suggesting downward occupational mobility of forward caste people is rare.[35] Some studies[36] indicate for intergenerational occupational and social mobility. The findings of such studies are outlined below.

Education and Mobility

Occupational and social mobility is associated with educational advancement. On the basis of Census figures from 1901 to 1931, N.K. Bose states: 'having a very low proportion of literate (1931: 4.52%) the Chamars and Mochis (leather-worker) have remained in their traditional occupation in a fair number, and the Kamars (blacksmith) having a higher proportion of literates (1931: 14.91%) than other artisan castes and because of their skills, even though their traditional occupations have declined, they have been able to turn to other industries without difficulty'.[37] Alexander (1968) pointed out *educational* achievement as one of the determining factors for social mobility of Pulaya ex-untouchables of Kerala.[38] Nijhawan (1971) has shown higher education along with other factors for occupational mobility.[39] Khan (1980) reported association of illiteracy to traditional occupations of low status and literacy beyond lower primary level to non-traditional occupations of high status.[40] Doshi (1980) observed *lack of educational ability among some of the Bhangis and the Nadias of Surat for their persuasion of conventional jobs*.[41] Mehra and others (1984) pointed out upward mobility among ex-untouchables of Haryana village as a result of expansion of education as one of the factors responsible for deviation from own caste occupation.[42] Thus, *educational advancement was found to be the crucial factor for occupational mobility*.

Impact of Industrial and Urban Growth

Some studies reported the impact of industrial and urban growth as a factor responsible for occupational mobility of persons from ex-untouchable background. Bose (1978) observed negative impact of leather industries for the ruination of Muchis' leather trade and adoption of wage-employment in agriculture and other industries.[43] Parmar (1978) has reported the establishment of modern industries as one of the factors of occupational change among the Mahyavanshis.[44] Doshi (1980) has undertaken a study on 500 Harijan households belonging to the six Harijan castes. The study revealed that 72.4 per cent of the Harijans were engaged in non-conventional jobs. Although Doshi has not examined such change, one can infer industrial-urban factor for it. In addition to occupational change, he pointed out it as a positive change towards the removal of untouchability as well.[45] Lapoint and Lapoint (1985) examined social mobility of Jatavs of a village in Meerut district. The findings suggested industrial and urban growth in surrounding Meerut and Delhi cities for their occupational change.[46] Indiresan and Gill (1985) observed very interesting and significant change of downward occupational mobility of forward caste people that they adopted jobs in leather industries. But, it pointed out that forward caste people were engaged in clean jobs and the ex-untouchable caste people in dirty jobs.[47] These studies indicates that occupational and interactional change have occurred as a result of *modern industrial* and *urban growth*.

Legislative and Governmental Welfare Measures

Since British India many legislative and governmental measures are introduced for the upliftment of scheduled castes people and removal of their disabilities created out of untouchability. Saberwal (1973) observed Balmikis (scavengers) and Ad Dharmis (shoemaker) who became leather-workers, entrepreneurs, contractors, teachers, farmers and bureaucrats. He pointed out the receding proportion of pollution among the intercaste relations in Modelpur town in Punjab. Such occupational and social mobility have occurred as a result of the Constitutional and the other legal measures and the rise of resistence by the persons from the lowest castes.[48] Santhakumari assessed the impact of the various governmental welfare programmes for the scheduled castes of Trivendrum district in Kerala. On the basis of her rural based study, she observed vertical occupational mobility, however, very limited.[49] Khan (1980) also conducted a study selecting 500 sample from villages in Bangalore district. He also observed little change and reported a little more than one-fifth of the respondents, who had taken up cultivation of lands.[50] These studies suggest *legislative* and *governmental welfare measures* as *more effective in urban setting* and less in rural.

Aspiration to Improve Status

Some studies reported a socio-psychological factor for mobility. While studying the trends of occupational mobility among scheduled castes in the six villages K.L. Sharma observed the motivation of discarding menial works among Chambhars, Naiks, Nais and Meenas. He analysed occupational mobility of lower castes 'for Sanskritizing their traditional life-ways and elevating their caste positions'.[51] Gangrade (1975) aimed at analysing social mobility comparatively among Chamars and Bhangis of Chattera village in the State of Haryana. He observed that most of them dissociated themselves from their traditional occupations. He discussed 'desire to improve their lot to attain a higher status' towards the most important factor contributing change, and other opportunities available to them as less important.[52] Kalam Singh (1984) investigated a phenomenon of intergenerational occupational mobility in the rural setting. In his study of six villages, he observed a tendency among the members of lower caste groups to adopt traditional occupations of higher caste groups and to move towards secular occupations. This movement is explained by the scholar in terms of "out-group socialization" (referred to class-based).[53] Thus, *psychological attributes* found to be contributed towards discarding the traditional occupations.

Different Mobility Patterns

Different mobility patterns are reported such as mobility at interactional level, diversion from traditional occupation to labour force and intergenerational mobility.

Alexander (1968) observed substantial changes between caste-Hindus and Pulayas at the interactional levels such as mode of addressing, using of abject words, house entry, services of barber and washerman, intercaste marriages, offering hospitality, etc. These changes occurred because Pulaya ex-untouchables improved themselves educationally and economically.[54] S.K. Sharma (1984) conducted a study of 126 workers engaged in the shoe industries. He has shown that 25 per cent respondents' friendship has crossed the caste line and it is taken as a sign of receding untouchability.[55]

Madan's (1966) Ladpur village study reveals that; Pasis and Chamars left their caste work and majority of them joined labour force.[56] L.P. Vidyarthi (1984) reported that some from Mehtars, Doms, Bhagtas and Ghasis in Bihar had left their traditional caste work and joined agricultural and other sectors of wage earning. He pointed out 'economic and social oppression and limited job opportunities' as the major causes for migration of scheduled castes.[57] I.P. Desai (1976) reported diversion from polluting activities in rural Gujarat.[58] Mehra and others (1984) reported upward mobility more among ex-untouchables than the upper castes. It indicated growth of service sector and advancement of the region as factors responsible for detaching caste from occupation.[59]

At the intergenerational level, in a comparative field study of rural Andhra, Lakshmanna (1973) reported that least deviation was among the Harijans (15.75%), followed by the upper caste non-Brahmins (17.44%).[60] In this way, mobility reveals at different levels.

Persuasion of Traditional Activity

Some studies reported no change in the traditional activity, especially of the lowest castes people due to their lack of educational advancement and the secured source of income of the job of scavenging and sweeping in the Municipal Communities. Sarkar (1984) informs that the sweepers in some Hill towns of North-East India belong to the tribes mostly.[61] But in Shillong the scavenging and sweeping have remained exclusively of Sikhs.[62] Even though author does not mention the caste-origin of those Sikhs, it clearly suggests from its discussion that they belonged to the untouchable caste originally and later got converted to Sikhism. The author discussed two different identities: one is that they affiliate themselves with a group of Sardar and the other identity from Sardar of Harijan for getting employment security.[63]

Another study also reveals the similar trend. In the empirical data of 1971, Shyamlal (1984) reports that; all, except two, of 82 household heads were still engaged in the traditional occupation of the sweepers to account the fact of caste and occupation association in case of Bhangis. He forwarded the evidence to this association by another study revealing that out of total of 957 employees, a large majority of 711 were engaged as sweepers and scavengers among the Bhangis in Rajasthan. In the same discussion, author mentioned another survey of Bhangis of Mysore; that 85 per cent were employed as sweepers. Moreover, author attempted to show the relationship of educational level and occupational activity. It is noticeable that 4 matriculates were also doing the same traditional activity.[64] In spite of the various governmental programmes and other diversified opportunities opened to the city Bhangis, no noteworthy occupational mobility is observed. Thus, *immobility* is identified by and large mostly among the *Bhangis*.

Studies at the Level of Maharashtra Region

Though very few studies on occupational and social mobility are available of Maharashtra region, however, are suggestive. The studies reported the significant changes in comparison with the other parts of India have accounted for the fact of social movements led by the reformers in Maharashtra.

Movement as Determinant of Mobility

An extensive widespread socio-economic survey of total 4,475 families of major ex-untouchable castes was undertaken at village level in Maharashtra by Gare and Limaye (1970). The findings of survey reported abandoning of traditional menial activities mostly from the families of the Mahars and the Neo-Buddhists throughout the parts of Maharashtra, and the families of the Mangs, the Chambhars, and the Dhors follow the next in order. Their castewise percentages reported respectively are 62, 68, 53, 35 and 29.[65] Thus the occupational mobility among the Neo-Buddhists or the Mahars is remarkable. The survey did not intend to examine the mobility, but it attributed to the influence of movements led by Dr. Babasaheb Ambedkar.

Sunanda Patwardhan (1973) conducted empirical study of ex-untouchables of Poona city to understand and determine the factors responsible for social mobility. It examined the factors such as occupation, education, religious conversion, migration, urbanization and social movements. The occupational sample covered six ex-untouchable castes, *viz.*, Mahar, Mang, Chambhar, Dhor, Bhangi and Holar. The important findings of the study are: (1) Chambhars and Dhors continued to carry out their hereditary profession, because they viewed it more profitable in the modern setting. (2) Mahars had given up traditional occupation in an urban area due to increasing literacy and higher education along with a rejection of the Hindu social system. (3) Urbanization indicates for greater occupational mobility, but the lowest castes people have not been able to gain any appreciable advantage by the impact of industrialization.[66]

A study of occupational pattern in two Marathwada villages shows the similar trend to the above. It reported that the Dhor families and a Chambhar were engaged in their traditional services.[67] Further it reported that all the Buddhist families (former Mahars) abandoned their traditional callings as a result of their conversion to Buddhism, and the Mangs also shifted to non-traditional occupations.[68]

In the recent study of Nagpur city, Rahate (1985) observed that the Mahars had left their traditional occupations totally, whereas Mehtars (scavengers) were not willing to leave their traditional job. They had to continue their activities as they did not possess other alternatives like educational qualification and other better means of livelihood to substitute their earlier ones.[69] The explanation given for change among the Mahars is that; they have become educated and also have become conscious of their derogatory menial works as a result of inspiration from Dr. Babasaheb Ambedkar.[70] Thus, factor of *social movements* led by the social reformers and social workers indicated as determinant for occupational and social mobility especially among the Mahars or later Neo-Buddhists and other lowest castes.

Summary

To sum up, one finds through the above mentioned studies at world level that class, race, wealth, family and religious background, and education are significant factors in relation to mobility. As a result of reformative legislations in favour of Negroes and Civil Rights Movement in the U.S., chances are increased to attain the upper mobility. In spite of opportunities to the Blacks, they are facing racial barriers in achieving the place in the upper strata. Hence, some limitations to mobility are bound to be there for some generations to pass. Also, a family background plays significant role to develop motivations and aspirations in achieving the occupational career.

National level studies have emphasized a relation between occupational and social mobility and pointed out the positive factors such as educational advancement, efforts through social movements, legislative and governmental welfare measures, impact of urban and industrial growth, aspiration to improve status; and also, the negative factors such as lack of occupational opportunities in rural setting, and the process of urbanization among the ex-untouchables due to their economic and social oppression. In case of scavengers and sweepers, there is a correspondence between caste and occupation which accounts for the reason of lack of educational advancement and the security of good income and a facility of housing accommodation in the local Municipal limit.

Lastly, the studies of Maharashtra region exclusively suggest the factor of different social movements led by the reformers, especially Dr. Ambedkar's movement of conversion of religion, which shows the influence among the Mahars.

REFERENCES

1. Krausz, Ernest: 'Factors of Social Mobility in British Minority Groups', *The British Journal of Sociology*, Vol. 23, 1972, p. 276.
2. Ibid.
3. Ibid., p. 278.
4. Ibid., p. 281.
5. Ibid., p. 280.
6. Ibid., p. 283.
7. Goldthorpe, J.H. and Llewellyn, C.: 'Class Mobility: Intergenerational and worklife patterns', *The British Journal of Sociology*, Vol. 28, No. 3, September 1977, pp. 269-302.
8. Erikson, Robert, Goldthorpe, J.H. and Portacarerol: 'Intergenerational Class Mobility in three Western European Societies: England, France and Sweden, *The British Journal of Sociology*, Vol. 30, No. 4, December 1979, p. 438.
9. Ibid.
10. Lieberson, S. and Fuguilt, G.V.: 'Negro-White Occupational Differences in the Absence of Discrimination', *American Journal of Sociology*, Vol. 73, No. 2, September 1967, p. 197.
11. Ibid.
12. Ransford, Edward, H. and Jeffries, Vincent: Social Stratification - a Multiple hierarchy approach, Allyn and Bacon, 1980, p. 156.
13. Ibid., p. 157.
14. Ibid.
15. Ibid., p. 174.
16. Ibid., p. 533.
17. Krausz, Ernest: *op. cit.,* p. 280.

18. Bendix and Lipset (ed.): Class, Status and Power, Free Press, 1966, p. 591.
19. Ibid., p. 592.
20. Ibid., pp. 582-601.
21. Kelley, Jonathan: 'Wealth and Family Background in the Occupational Career', *The British Journal of Sociology*, Vol. 29, No. 1, March 1978, p. 98.
22. Ibid., p. 106.
23. Lin, N. and Yauger, D.: 'The Process of Occupational Status Achievement', *American Journal of Sociology*, Vol. 81, No. 3, November 1975, p. 556.
24. Ibid., p. 579.
25. Jackson, F.E., Fox, W.S. and Crockett, Jr.: 'Religion and Occupational Achievement', *American Sociological Review*, Vol. 35, No. 1, 1970, p. 51.
26. Ibid., p. 60.
27. Kerckhoff, A.C., Campbell, R.T. and Trott, J.M.: 'Dimensions of Educational and Occupational Attainment in Great Britain', *American Sociological Review*, Vol. 47, June 1982, p. 360.
28. Kelley, Jonathan: *op. cit.;* p. 101.
29. Treiman, Donald J. and Terrell, Kermit: 'The Process of Status Attainment in the United States and Great Britain', *American Journal of Sociology*, Vol. 81, No. 3, 1975, p. 579.
30. Madan, G.R.: *India's Social Transformation,* Vol. I, Allied, New Delhi, 1979, p. 218.
31. Lapoint, E.C. and Lapoint, D.N.: 'Socio-Economic Mobility Among Village Harijans', *The Eastern Anthropologist*, Vol. 38, No. 1, January-February 1985.
32. Santhakumari, R.: *Scheduled Caste and Welfare Measures,* Classical Publishing Company, New Delhi.
33. Doshi, Harish: 'Occupational Diversification and Removal of Untouchability', in *Removal of Untouchability;* Shah, V.P. (ed.); Sociology Deptt., Gujarat University, Ahmedabad, 1980.
34. (a) Sarkar, Jayanta: *Caste, Occupation and Change,* B.R. Publishing, Delhi, 1984.
    (b) Shyamlal: Chap.: *Caste, and Occupational Mobility: The Bhangis in transition*, Inter-India, New Delhi, 1984.
    (c) Desai, I.P.: *Untouchability in Rural Gujarat,* Popular Prakashan, Bombay, 1976.
35. Indiresan, Jayalakshmi and Gill, Shiela: 'Social Change Among Leather Artisans', *Social Change*, Vol. 15, No. 1, March 1985.
36. (a) Singh, Soran: 'Occupational Mobility Among Scheduled Castes', *The Indian Journal of Social Work*, Vol. XXXVII, No. 3, October 1976.
    (b) Singh, Kalam: 'Occupational Mobility in Rural Setting', *The Indian Journal of Social Research*, Vol. XXV, No. 2, 1984.
    (c) Phillips, W.S.K.: 'Social Structure and Mobility in an Urban Setting'; *Social Action*, April-June, Vol. 30, No. 2, 1980.
    (d) Lakshmanna, C.: *Caste Dynamics in Village India*, Nachiketa, 1973.
    (e) Alexander, K.C.: 'Changing Status of Pulaya Harijans of Kerala'; *Economic and Political Weekly*, Special Number, July 1968.
    (f) Sharma, Satish Kumar: 'Traditional Occupational Skills and Social Mobility'; Paper presented at *XVII All India Sociological Conference*, held at Surat, 1984.
37. Bose, N.K.: *The Structure of Hindu Society* (trans.), Sangam Books, 1976, p. 51.
38. Alexander, K.C.: *op. cit.;* p. 321.
39. Nijhawan, N.K.: 'Occupational Mobility and Political Development', *Economic and Political Weekly*, Annual Number, Vol. VI, January 1971, p. 321.

40. Khan, Mumtaz Ali: *Scheduled Castes and Their Status in India*, Uppal Publishing House, New Delhi, 1980, p. 128.
41. Doshi, Harish: *op. cit.*.
42. Mehra, Savita, Sharma, M.L. and Dak, T.M.: 'Changing Correspondence between Caste and Occupation: a socio-economic analysis, *The Eastern Anthropologist*, Vol. 37, No. 4, October-December 1984, p. 335.
43. Bose, N.K.: *op. cit.;* p. 152.
44. Parmar, Y.A.: 'Occupational Change Among Mahyavanshis - a Scheduled Caste', *The Indian Journal of Social Work*, vol. XXXIX, October 1978, pp. 228-237.
45. Doshi, Harish: *op. cit.*.
46. Lapoint, E.C. and Lapoint, D.N.: *op. cit.*.
47. Indiresan, Jayalakshmi and Gill, Shiela: 'Social Change Among Leather Artisans': *Social Change*, Vol. 15, No. 1, March 1985.
48. Saberwal, S.: 'Receding Pollution: Intercaste Relations in Punjab', *Sociological Bulletin*, Vol. 22, 1973, pp. 234-259.
49. Santhakumari, R.: *op. cit.;* pp. 98-102.
50. Khan, Mumtaz Ali: *op. cit.;* p. 127.
51. Sharma, K.L.: *The Changing Rural Stratification System*, Orient Longman, 1974, pp. 156-168.
52. Gangrade, K.D.: 'Social Mobility in India: A Study of depressed class', *Man in India*, Vol. 55, 3, September, 1975, p. 252.
53. Singh, Kalam: *op. cit.*, p. 216.
54. Alexander, K.C.: *op. cit.*.
55. Sharma, Satish Kumar: *op. cit.*.
56. Madan, G.R.: *op. cit.*.
57. Vidyarthi, L.P.: 'Position and Problems of Scheduled Castes in Bihar', *The Eastern Anthropologist*, Vol. 37, No. 3, July-September 1984, pp. 281-285.
58. Desai, I.P.: *op. cit.;* p. 162.
59. Mehra, Savita, Sharma, M.L. and Dak, T.M.: 'Changing Correspondence Between Caste and Occupation: A Socio-economic Analysis', *The Eastern Anthropologist*, Vol. 37, No. 4, October-December 1984, p. 335.
60. Lakshmanna, C.: *op. cit.;* p. 99.
61. Sarkar, Jayanta: *op. cit.;* p. 59.
62. Ibid., p. 71.
63. Ibid.
64. Shyamlal: *op. cit.;* pp. 32-39.
65. Gare, Govind and Limaye, Shirubhau: *Maharashtratil Dalit-Shodh aani Bodh (Marathi);* Sahadhyaya Prakashan, Bombay, 1970, pp. 68, 82, 92, 106, 120, 133, 144, 158, 166.
66. Patwardhan, Sunanda: *Change Among India's Harijans*, Orient Longman, 1973, p. 203.
67. Kulkarni, M.G. and Hiramani, A.B.: 'Occupational Pattern in two Marathwada Villages - a comparative study'; *Marathwada University Journal*, Vol. XIV, No. 2, September 1975, p. 93.
68. Ibid., pp. 96 and 97.
69. Rahate, J.V.: Modernization among Scheduled Castes with special reference to Mahars, Weavers and Sweepers of Nagpur city (Marathi); Ph.D. dissertation (unpublished), Marathwada University, Aurangabad, 1985, p. 188.
70. Ibid., p. 198.

THREE

Research Design and Data Collection

Introduction

As discussed in the previous chapter, a number of studies evidenced occupational mobility among scheduled castes people. But none of the studies focussed solely on self-employment occupations and the persons engaged in it. As occupational opportunities are more in urban setting, Kolhapur city is selected for the purpose of the study. Historically, Kolhapur is known for Shahu Chhatrapati's revolutionary role for providing not only educational facilities to the ex-untouchables, but some of them were given financial and other help also to enter into the self-employment. In this background, it is intended to study the adoption of self-employed jobs by those of ex-untouchable persons. The respondents are selected from both traditional and modern categories of occupations to pin-point the factors for the adoption of modern occupations. Moreover, occupational mobility is considered as an independent variable to examine social mobility. In addition, the focus of the study is to identify the factors helpful for both occupational and social mobility. To study such mobility, the research design which was adopted, is stated below.

Objectives of the Study

The general objective is to examine the sources of occupational mobility together with its consequences on their social status in the changing structure of society.

The specific objectives of this study are:

(1) To investigate the different sources of occupational mobility and especially the motivational sources.

(2) To identify the different types of modern occupations adopted by those of ex-untouchable persons.

(3) To examine the impact of occupational mobility on the removal of untouchability at commensal level.
(4) To identify occupational mobility by variables such as caste, religion, education, age, sex and family background.
(5) To assess the efforts of ex-untouchables towards their success in occupational activities.
(6) To measure the social status of the respondents as an individual and his family as a result in adoption of modern economic activities as compared to the status of those persons who are still engaged in their traditional occupations.
(7) To find out reasons for the occupational immobility of the respondents engaged in caste jobs.
(8) To compare social mobility of those who adopted modern occupations with that of those who did not.
(9) To identify the emergence of entrepreneurs among scheduled castes during Post-Independent industrial-urban setting.

Hypotheses

To assess both occupational and social mobility, the following hypotheses are formulated:

(1) The persons who have adopted occupations which are not regarded contemptuous removes the stigma of untouchability and such persons become acceptable to the upper caste-Hindus for interactions.
(2) The social status of a person raises along with the economic status.
(3) The policies and the programmes of Shahu Chhatrapati to uplift the untouchables helped them towards occupational and social mobility.
(4) The self-respect movement led and steered by Dr. Ambedkar among ex-untouchables motivated them towards occupational mobility.
(5) The opening of educational complex in the rural Western Maharashtra by Karmaveer Bhaurao Patil created a source of inspiration among some ex-untouchables in adopting the self-employed jobs.

(6) The urban way of life has become the source of motivation to the ex-untouchables for shunning away their caste-based traditional occupations.
(7) The special support by kins and relatives enabled the ex-untouchable persons towards the adoption of modern economic activities.
(8) The principal assistance rendered by the Mahatma Phule Backward Class Development Corporation and other agencies made ex-untouchable persons conscious of choosing self-employed jobs.
(9) The modern educational, political and interactional opportunities have become available due to the antidisabilities and compensatory legislation in post-Independent India which encouraged the class of ex-untouchables for occupying a place in the self-respectable jobs.
(10) An access to service opportunities in the Christian Missionary Institutions gave way to the new life chances of education and service jobs mostly to those who belonged to the caste of an untouchable.

Selection of an Area of the Study

Occupational restrictions have been the discernible feature of caste system in India. Since British rule in India, some channels for occupational mobility have been opened at least in urban centres. The interplay of modern processes like formal education, bureaucratic administration, industrialization, urbanization and secularization in twentieth century helped in many ways for mobility. During post-Independent period, day by day occupational mobility among scheduled caste people is seen increasing in service sector. Their mobility in self-employed occupations is also visible. With the growth of industries and markets whether some ex-untouchables could mobilize towards self-employment jobs, and if so, what made them possible to adopt it, suggested me to examine the mobility of such people.

There are other reasons also to examine their mobility. They do not inherit the background of entrepreneurship as it is among the Jains, the Gujars, and the Marwadis. Also, they do not inherit a wealth for capital investment. Even if one dares to start a hotel, one is not sure of getting customers due to the prevalence of the notion of untouchability. But, this situation appears to be changed at least in urban setting. In city many of the interactions take place at secular level. The behaviour of people in urban community is regulated by legal-rational norms. In such a background, to what extent occupational mobility has become possible is also the purpose of study.

Selection of Universe

Focus of the study is occupational mobility of self-employed individuals engaged in varied occupations. The individuals employed in government administration or in teaching service are not considered, it is because they are employed by virtue of the Constitutional provisions of the reservation facilities. Here, self-employed are considered for the reasons that they have chosen those occupations where they can work independently as masters of their activities.

For the selection of the respondents, stratified and purposive sampling types are used. Accordingly, 200 respondents engaged in modern occupations, and in contrast 30 respondents engaged in their own caste traditional jobs, are selected from the five castes *viz.*, Mahar, Mang, Dhor, Chambhar and Bhangi. A purposive sample is selected by the knowledge that the individuals who are self-employed, are identified by their caste to some of their customers and also to some persons in the locality of residence.

As many as two hundred respondents from the five castes are selected for sample so that it would cover the different categories of occupations. In contrast, the researcher confined to 30 respondents from the five castes engaged in their hereditary occupations. It is for the reason that each of the five castes has its limited occupational categories. And, also, for the reason that the responses from the respondents of caste-jobs were not varying.

Selection of Sub-groups

Five castes from ex-untouchable groups are selected for the study purpose. These castes are Mahar, Mang, Dhor, Chambhar and Bhangi. These five castes are popularly known as major groups of untouchable origin. Moreover, these are selected because, first four are from village community and a Bhangi caste from urban community in the Maharashtra region.

Selection of Unit: Kolhapur City

Shahu's Foundation for Modernisation

Historically, Kolhapur is famous as a State of Chhatrapatis. Before the ascendence of Shahu as Chhatrapati, some important developments were already made by previous Chhatrapati. Rajaram College was established in 1880. A Technical Institute for engineering and industrial education was established in 1887. The rail road from Kolhapur to Miraj was constructed in 1891. At present, three express trains run daily from Kolhapur to Bombay.

In 1894 Shahu ascended the throne as Chhatrapati. He laid the foundation of overall developments in education, social, industrial, etc. He laid the foundation of hostel in 1896 and opened 23 hostels till 1921 for the students of all castes. In 1893-94 the total number of educational institutions (Primary to College) were 224 and it rose to 559 in the year 1921-22. In 1893-94 there were 14,819 students taking education and in 1921-22 the number rose to 31,096.[1] Agricultural Institute was also established at Kolhapur in 1912-13. Industrial and Agricultural Exhibition was also held in 1914.[2] The growth of untouchable pupils is remarkable. During 1894 the enrolment of untouchable students was 234 only, but in 1921-22 by the end of Shahu's rule it rose to 2,162.[3]

Shahu was a social revolutionary. At his own level, first he himself became radical against the tyranny of Brahminism. He introduced the number of social legislation including inter-religion and inter-caste marriages, etc. He welcomed the Satya Shodhak Samaj (truth-seeker society) to educate the non-Brahmin masses and the Christian Missionaries to provide health and educational services to the poor. He provided help and encouraged them. Some social and political workers were influenced by Shahu's inspiration. Some were prominent namely, Madhavrao Bagal and Bhaskarrao Jadhav from Maratha, and D.S. Powar and Gangaram Kamble from ex-untouchable castes of Chambhar and Mahar respectively. What Shahu did for the emancipation of ex-untouchables is stated in detail in Appendix II.

For the growth of trade and industries, Shahu made a number of infrastructural developments such as water works and roads for transportation. He built dams, tanks and wells for irrigation. Radhanagari and Kalammawadi are the examples of dams. He constructed a large number of roads connecting villages and towns with Kolhapur. These link-roads ultimately encouraged the trade and commerce in Kolhapur and its region. Shahu Chhatrapati started the Cooperative movement. The Cooperative Act was passed for the first time in 1904.[4] In 1912-13 Shahu established first the Urban Cooperative Credit Society.[5] Shahu had laid a foundation of spinning and weaving Mills in 1906 and it is named after him. In the same Mills 1,940 workers are working and among them 371 workers (i.e., 19.12 per cent) are from the Scheduled Castes.[6] It indicates a more number of Scheduled Castes if compared to their population percentage i.e., 11.6. Shahu had laid foundation of Gur Market in Kolhapur City. In 1933 Rajaram Maharaj, then Chhatrapati of Kolhapur founded Sugar Mill at Bavada village near Kolhapur.

Thus, Shahu's educational and industrial policies generated the progress of industrialization and urbanization. His developments contributed considerably to the present establishment of spinning and weaving mills, oil engines, oil mills, foundaries, automobiles, and consequently caused the background for the development of interactional relationships down to the ex-untouchables.

Population Composition

According to 1981 Census, the population of Kolhapur City is 3,40,625. Its decadal growth since 1901 is shown in Table 3.1 General population figures indicate for its slower growth but in comparison with 1971 Census, the Scheduled Caste population is increased from 8.70 per cent to 11.06 per cent in 1981.

According to 1971 Census the distribution of religionwise population is shown in Table 3.2.

The figures of Table 3.2 clearly indicate for the majority of the Hindus and the rest of the religion-population for their minority.

Table 3.3 indicates lower literacy growth among Scheduled Castes in its comparison.

Urban community is generally characterised by a heterogeneous population, an exercise of formal social control, a prevalence of impersonal, secondary and secular relations. These general characteristics, undoubtedly, hold true with Kolhapur city.

TABLE 3.1: **Kolhapur City classified by population in 1981 with variation**

Year	Persons	Decade variation	Percentage of Decade variation	Scheduled castes
1901	54,374	-	-	-
1911	42,018	-12,355	-22.72	-
1921	52,299	+10,281	+24.47	-
1931	66,728	+14,429	+27.59	-
1941	93,032	+26,304	+39.42	-
1951	136,835	+43,803	+47.08	-
1961	187,442	+50,607	+36.98	-
1971	259,050	+70,608	+38.20	22,788* (8.79%)
1981	340,625	+81,575	+31.49	37,692** (11.06%)

Source: Census of India, 1981, Series-12, Maharashtra, Part II-A, General Population Tables, p. 174.
* Census of India 1971, Series-11, Maharashtra, Part II-C (i), Social & Cultural Tables, p. 210.
** Census of India, 1981, Series-12, Maharashtra, Part-II-B, Primary Census Abstract, p. 56.

TABLE 3.2: **Kolhapur City classified by religion**

Religion	Persons	Percentage
Hindu	2,19,773	84.83
Muslim	25,450	9.82
Jain	9,468	3.65
Christian	3,409	1.31
Buddhist	666	0.25
Sikh	263	0.10
Other religions	12	0.004
Religion not stated	9	0.003
Total population	2,59,050	100.00

Source: Census of India 1971, Series-11, Maharashtra, Part-II C(i), Social and Cultural Tables, pp. 56-7.

TABLE 3.3: **Kolhapur City classified by literate population**

Category	Total persons	Literate persons	Percentage
Total population	3,40,625 (100%)	2,27,656*	66.83
Scheduled castes	37,692 (11.06%)	17,546**	46.55

Source: * Census of India 1981, Series-12, Maharashtra, Paper-1 of 1981, Supplement, p. 123.
** Census of India 1981, Series-12, Maharashtra, Part-2 of 1982, Primary Census Abstract, Scheduled Castes and Scheduled Tribes, p. 47.

Pattern of Residence in Kolhapur City

According to 1981 Census, the area of Kolhapur Corporation is 66.82 Kilometre with 61,236 residential houses.[7] The present Corporation Council is composed of 60 Councillors elected from 60 Wards. A remarkable feature is that two Councillors belonging to Mang and Mahar castes were elected in the Corporation election held in February 1985 from the general category, namely, Dr. Sudam Chaugule (a respondent of this study) and Jalindar Pawar. Dr. Chaugule who got twice elected from Rajarampuri Ward, a ward of upper middle class and upper caste-Hindus. Such thing is rarely witnessed elsewhere. This change can be illustrated for the secular characteristic of the city.

So far there are 19 smaller and bigger localities known for most of those people belonging to the sub-groups of ex-untouchable category. These localities are scattered in different parts of the city. Some upper caste-Hindus, however, few live in the localities which are known for the dwelling houses of ex-untouchable groups and *vice-versa*. Moreover, the researcher is informed that there are dwelling houses of middle and upper caste-Hindus in the Housing Societies, namely, Jawaharnagar, Sadar Bazar, Bhim Vijaya, and Shastrinagar. The inter-mixture pattern of dwelling houses of upper caste-Hindus and ex-untouchables produces varied interactions

Industrial Developments

According to 1981 Census, Kolhapur city is classified as industrial and commercial for its functional category. The city has maintained its continuous industrial growth. In 1945 Ghatage-Patil firm started with goods transport and now it contributed to its large scale industrial development with motor spare parts products and repair workshop. In Kolhapur city and its agglomeration some industrial zones are developed, namely, Shivaji Uddyamnagar in the heart of the city and the Maharashtra Industrial Development Corporation at Shiroli and Gokulshirgaon on Pune-Bangalore Highway.

According to the Directorate of Industries, 24 large and medium scale industries, 963 small scale industries till 1977 and 267 in 1978-79 are registered[8] as industrial and engineering units in Kolhapur city and its agglomeration. Some of the major products of these industrial and engineering Units are malted food, automobile spare-parts, cotton yarn and cloth, sugar, piston and piston rings, diesel and oil engines, oil engine spare-parts, leather and foot-wear, agricultural implements, chemicals, repairs of lathes and electric motors, steel furniture, printing machinery, etc.

Growth of Workers and Other Professionals

This industrial growth influenced the growth of main workers in Kolhapur city. The growth of main workers in total and of Scheduled Castes also is presented in Table 3.4.

TABLE 3.4: **Growth of Main Workers in Kolhapur city**

Year	Total Main Workers	Scheduled Castes
1961*	53,060	4,265 (8.03%)
1981	84,181 **	10,916 @ (12.96%)

Source: * Census of India 1961, Vol. X, Maharashtra, Part X (2-12), Cities of Maharashtra Census Tables, pp. 412, and 462.
** Census of India 1981, Series-I, Part II B (i), Primary Census Abstract, General Population, p. 320.
@ Census of India 1981, Series-12, Maharashtra, Paper 2 of 1982, Scheduled Castes and Scheduled Tribes, Primary Census Abstract, p. 48.

The above growth of workers from Scheduled Castes in 1981 is represented more i.e., 12.96 per cent as main workers in proportion to the general population. And, according to 1981 Census in Kolhapur city 3,462[9] persons were engaged in household industries (manufacturing, processing and repairs) and among them 466[10] persons were from the Scheduled Castes. In household industries the representation of Scheduled Caste workers is more i.e., 13.46 per cent to their population proportion i.e., 11.06. The Census category of Household Industry does not specify its type. As Kolhapur is known for leather industry, it might have been caused to swell the figure due to the age-old associationship of the Dhors and the Chambhars to their leather activities.

In Kolhapur District the total population of all types of motor vehicles was 67,916 as on dt. 31.3.1985.[11] It generates more scope in Kolhapur city since it is a central place for self-employment such as spare-parts shop proprietary, auto-mechanic and transportation service.

Kolhapur District is famous for dairy-farming also. During 1984-85, as much as 4,19,15,160 litres milk was collected by the Kolhapur District Cooperative Milk Producers Society with its working capital Rs. 13,01,29,258.[12] According to the private Survey[13] undertaken in 1983 there were 85 private and cooperative milk distributors in Kolhapur city.

In order to visualize the entry of ex-untouchable persons into the self-employment sector, the figures of some professionals are considered in the study. Only those who are registered in the office of the local Municipal Corporation, the figures of those professionals are stated in Table 3.5.

TABLE 3.5: **Professionals (Licensee) in Kolhapur city as on November 1985**

Sr. No.	Occupational category		Professionals
1	Tea Hotel	...	448
2	Boarding houses	...	288
3	Confectionery	...	225
4	Dairies	...	108
5	Grocery: a. retail	...	1,509
	b. wholesale	...	732
6	Gur (wholesale)	...	230
7	Pan-Cigar sellers	...	991
8	Shoe-makers' shops	...	174
9	Firewood stalls	...	283
10	Laundries	...	235
	Total:		5203

Source: Shri C.A. Mohite, Licence Superintendent, Kolhapur Corporation.

About 430 Advocates were enrolled as members of the Kolhapur Bar Council as on November 1985.[14] The Sales-Tax and the Income-Tax Consultants and also the Chartered Accounts were approximately 325[15] as on dt. 28.2.1986 in Kolhapur city. The independent Architect Practitioners were approximately 125.[16] There were 472[17] Medical general practitioners and consultants in the city.

Financing Agencies

In Kolhapur city the major offices of financing agencies are established such as the State Industrial and Investment Corporation of

Maharashtra (SICOM), the Maharashtra State Finance Corporation (MSFC), the Mahatma Phule Backward Class Development Corporation (MPBCDC), 109[18] branches of the Nationalised, the Scheduled and the Cooperative Banks, the District Industrial Centre and other agencies. In all these agencies, the MP BCDC remained most useful to the Scheduled Castes persons. The details of castewise beneficiaries and the activitywise are given in Appendix IV.

Educational Institutions

Kolhapur is the seat of Shivaji University. In the city there are varied vocational institutions such as technical, industrial, engineering, polytechnic, animal husbandry, agriculture, photography, arts, typewriting, tailoring, cooperation, office management, banking, law, commerce, and so on.[19] It not only caters to the need of industrial workers but creates self-employment also.

Youth Clubs

The formation of youth clubs in all localities is certainly a unique feature of the city. The Youth Clubs take interest in the cultural activities and other day-to-day events. By way of such a club again interactions take place beyond one's caste or religion level among the youths and their family members subsequently.

Summary

The above discernible features of Kolhapur city can be concluded as inducing factors for both occupational and social mobility to the population of the community. In many respects Shahu Chhatrapati's role played a great deal as the foundation for modernisation.

In proportion to general population growth, the growth of Scheduled Castes population appears to be more. The residential pattern is marked of inter-mixture type which gives rise to the interactions at different levels. The city has become the complex of industrial and engineering units.

In all financing agencies, the Mahatma Phule Backward Class Development Corporation is the major source of financial assistance to the Scheduled Castes persons. The help given through it, however, is meagre.

The industrial growth influenced the growth of workers' population in general and in particular Scheduled Castes too. The general population growth, increasing population of vehicles, the development of dairy-farming, the growth of trade and commerce, and many other developments influenced the self-employment pattern. In such self-employment sector how many are from the Scheduled Castes category is difficult to ascertain. But, in general, in the process of high growth in modern economy and other developments, the entry of Scheduled Castes into it appears to be very marginal.

Tools and Data Collected

Primary Data

To approach the probable respondents, initially a list of about 400 proposed persons engaged in clean activities was prepared through the help of personal friends. For the information of respondents, the researcher visited each locality of an ex-untouchable groups and approached social activists belonging to the groups of ex-untouchable origin.

Meanwhile, the Interview Schedule was prepared for interviewing the proposed respondents engaged in clean activities. In the beginning the Interview Schedule was prepared after testing the 20 of the proposed respondents. After pre-testing it, some alterations were made in the Schedule. Inspite of some earlier modifications, while interviewing the respondents, the researcher had to add some alternative items of choice. For interviewing the persons engaged in traditional activities, a separate schedule was used by dropping some of the items which were not applicable to the respondents of caste-jobs category. For finalisation of the second instrument the similar procedure like the first Schedule was adopted. Thus, the separate instruments were used for interviewing the persons from both occupational categories of modern and the caste jobs.

Items of choice in the Schedule, although structured, were unstructured for the respondents. So, it were subject to a certain modifications without altering the substance of the subject. The freedom was given to the respondents to answer the questions asked by the researcher. To get a clue to respond, some of the alternatives from the Schedule were to be told to the respondents.

To interview the respondents, the researcher himself approached the proposed respondents. As the researcher has some involvement in certain social activities of the ex-untouchable groups, it could be possible to approach some of the respondents directly.

For interviewing them, the researcher preferred the home place of the respondents rather than the place of their work and in some cases left at the choice of the respondents. The reason to prefer home place was that of the information concerning the respondents' other family members' interactions with outsiders and also the information to be confirmed of their parents' jobs from the senior members of the family. In experience, this strategy was found to be useful.

For approaching the respondents, the researcher had taken the help of others. Instead of approaching the respondents directly, researcher used to approach first the proper source. Even then under the pretext of suspense three of the respondents did not respond to the interview properly. So the interview of such respondents was cancelled. Very few of the respondents were found unable to answer the questions. In such cases, interview was cancelled due to the inability of the respondents' poor grasp. In some cases, the respondents who belonged to the category of the Income-Tax payers have told their income less than the real. Some were not income-tax payers but in reality they were high income earners and they also told their income less than their real earning. While interviewing, in most of the cases, somebody was to be with me who was to be known to many of the things of the respondents.

To mention about the time consumed by an average respondent, was not less than 25 minutes. In respect of many of the respondents it consumed about one hour.

In general, an interview experience was much interesting and useful. Most of the respondents themselves enthusiastically cooperated the researcher. In many of the cases, an interview was found to be informal. There might be rare scope for bias except the item of income. Thus, the researcher is pleased to state that the information supplied by the respondents is objectively authentic.

The collection of data for the persons engaged in modern occupations started from the month of May, 1984 and completed by the end of November, 1984 and for the persons, who were engaged in caste-based occupations started and completed it in the month of April, 1985.

Secondary Data

The secondary source of data can be enlisted as under:

(1) The published Books on Shahu Chhatrapati, and the old paper files relating to Shahu Chhatrapati from the Office of Archives, Kolhapur are referred to the historical and foundational background of ex-untouchables' occupational and social mobility.
(2) The Kolhapur District Gazetteers are referred to the historical background of the city. The back issues of periodicals of Kolhapur Church Council are used for the background of the converted Christians and also the varied services of the Christian Missionaries.
(3) The Census Reports are used for population figures.
(4) The Industrial Directory published by the Government of Maharashtra is used for a number of industrial units.
(5) The office bearers of the different professional associations are met for the figures of the professionals.
(6) The office of the Kolhapur Municipal Corporation is consulted for the figures of the professionals, the scavengers and the sweepers, and for a copy of the City Map also.
(7) The office of the Mahatma Phule Backward Class Development Corporation, Regional Office, Kolhapur, is consulted for the data of beneficiaries from the groups of Scheduled Castes.
(8) For a copy of the Sanad and a photocopy of Dr. Ambedkar with a family, some individual sources are visited.
(9) The researcher had an interview with some Dalit social workers and the Christian priests to understand the spirit of mobility in Kolhapur city.

Definitions of Concepts and Terms

The concepts and the terms used in this study are defined below:

Occupational Mobility

Generally, the occupational mobility is conceived as the movement from the occupational category to another, i.e., manual to non-manual, semi-skilled to skilled, and likewise. Fox and Miller emphasised on ranking occupations by prestige levels rather than by indicators of skill, income, or span of control.[20] Hauser and Featherman proposed that in capitalist, industrial and other societies 'the common structure of social mobility is occupational socio-economic status'.[21] On the basis of review of occupational studies, they concluded 'socio-economic bases' to occupational mobility.[22] So here, prestige and socio-economic status are taken into account as the attributes of occupational mobility.

Social Mobility

Sorokin defines social mobility 'as a social phenomenon refers to a change or alteration in status of an individual or a group'.[23] He classified mobility into horizontal and vertical. By vertical mobility he meant 'the relations involved in a transition of an individual (or a social object) from one social stratum to another'.[24] According to the Dictionary of Sociology 'social mobility refers to the movement of individuals between different levels of the social hierarchy, usually defined occupationally'.[25] This defined version of change in status in the social hierarchy is quite clear towards the meaning of social mobility.

The Study of Social Mobility

Tumin discussed the study of social mobility. In it, he includes the reasons of sources, the patterns, and the consequences of movement.[26] For the study of social mobility, he considered some dimensions; such as dimension of time for intergenerational or intragenerational (career) mobility, dimension of systems of mobility in the context of occupational or educational as resources, dimension of mechanism of mobility concerning attainment of ascription or achievement, dimension of unit of mobility such as individuals or families or groups or strata, and aspects of change in status concerning income as an objective aspect and individual's feelings as to whether one considers it an improvement as subjective aspect of change.[27] To measure mobility, Tumin asserted over some of the aspects: (i) prestige aspect, e.g., economic, educational, or occupational, (ii) experiences for analysis, e.g., individuals', families', strata's, (iii) unit of comparison, e.g., fathers with sons, groups of persons considering time dimension, (iv) starting point, e.g., first job or activity itself as it is at the age category, and (v) classification of occupations along with income, educational levels, or with categories of strata such as sex, class, etc.[28] These dimensions and aspects are to be conceived certainly in the study of social mobility.

The Untouchables

For the definition of 'untouchables' I prefer to quote Dr. B.R. Ambedkar. He defined it in the notional sense that; 'an untouchable is a person who is seemed to belong to a class which is commonly held to cause pollution by touch'.[29] The notions of pollution are developed against the persons belonging to the impure castes, and prohibiting rules and restrictions are observed against the contacts of those persons to the objects; such as vessels and utensils, courtyard of a temple, a sitting floor, an interior of a house, a place in a locality or a residence of caste-Hindu, a food and the like.

The Scheduled Castes

According to the Art. 366(24) of the Constitution "Scheduled Castes" means such castes, races or tribes or parts of our groups within such castes, races or tribes as are deemed under article 341[30] to be Scheduled Castes for the purposes of this Constitution.[31] In fact, Scheduled Caste is a legal jargon coined by the British Government and later adopted by the Government of India in the Constitution for the purpose of special measures to be extended in the interest of those Castes. Professor Lelah Dushkin is right in commenting on it that: 'The term is appropriate only in this context of legal provisions, government action, and politics'.[32] Thus, the term 'Scheduled Castes' has legal context.

The Harijans

The term 'Harijan' is used by Mahatma Gandhi to the untouchables. The term 'Untouchable' is regarded derogatory in its use. Therefore, now, the term 'Harijan' has become popular to address the untouchables.

The Christians, the Buddhists and the Muslims

Generally, the Christians and the Muslims are undoubtedly identified different from the Hindus. But the Buddhists who are converted from the Hindus are still identified as a sub-section of the Hindus.

Some clarification is required about the Christians. The Census of India provides the information of population of Christian religion. It does not inform the caste of the converted Christians. The history of Indian Christians is the history of conversion. Generally, it is said that conversion took place mostly from the people of untouchable castes. The same is the truth of Kolhapur Christian Converts. In this regard, Missionaries' own publication, 'Western India Notes' reported that, 'wherever large numbers of people have become Christians, it has been from the lower caste or out-caste people'.[33] In the same brochure the dissatisfaction is expressed over the result of the evangelistic work that: 'Whatever conversions there were in this area due to missionary activity were from among the backward communities, particularly the two communities of the Mahar and the Mang, and the evangelistic work in this area is still limited to these two communities'.[34] It is confirmed from Mr. Panhalkar, the priest of Kolhapur Diocesan Council that; 44 out of the total 51 priests of the 44 church places have a background of origin of untouchable castes. Thus, it clearly reveals that the converted Christians in the Kolhapur region are mostly from the Mahars and the Mangs.

About the Muslims, it is well-known that conversion took place long back in the past. It is again well-known fact that during recent years few events of Muslim conversion are reported in the newspapers and the periodicals. Such event occurred in Kolhapur at individual level and rare individuals from the *Bhangis* are *converted to Muslim* religion.

The Ex-untouchables

The term 'ex-untouchables' is used by the scholars in their writings to address the untouchables whose origin is regarded from the groups of the untouchable castes.

Removal of Untouchability and Social Elevation

According to Dr. B.R. Ambedkar 'removal of untouchability' means 'to be free from the restrictions of marriage, food, water and touch',[35] and 'social elevation' means 'to be fit for respect and friendship.[36]

Clean Occupations

In the traditional conception of Hindu society, commonly, the clean occupations are regarded non-polluting occupations.

Elementary Education

The term elementary education is used in the Interview Schedule. The Dictionary of Education defines elementary education from I to VIII standard.[37] The dictionary of educational terms published by Government of India also defines elementary education upto VIII standard.[38]

Operational Definitions

The operational definitions for the present study are laid down as under:

Occupational Mobility

The adoption of modern or clean occupations (such as tailoring, mechanic, transport, advocacy, medical practice, and the like) by the persons from ex-untouchable origin is considered as occupational mobility to them. In this present study educational qualification, financial assistance, occupational experience and training are taken into account as the sources of occupational mobility. In this study, the adoption of modern occupation and the intergenerational occupational mobility from polluting to non-polluting occupations or from one modern occupation to another modern one by the persons from the next generations are considered as the levels of the occupational mobility towards its dimension.

Social Mobility

To measure social mobility, commensality or interactional relations in matters of friendship and participation in ritual occasions between a upper caste – Hindu and an ex-untouchable is considered as the major indice in the study. The respondent as an individual and his family as well are considered as the units of social mobility.

The Ex-untouchables

The term 'ex-untouchable(s)' is used in this dissertation as synonymous to the terms *viz.*, Harijans, Scheduled Castes, Untouchables and Depressed Class people.

The Christians, the Buddhists and the Muslims

Some converts from the Christians, the Buddhists and the Muslims are selected as respondents, whose origin is recognised from the ex-untouchable castes. The converts are selected only those who identify themselves with their caste origin and many of the caste-Hindus who are aware of their caste origin too. The criterion for identification adopted, is based on the information of the converts' caste-brethren.

The Untouchable Castes

The five castes *viz.*, Mahar, Mang, Dhor, Chambhar and Bhangi are considered as untouchable castes.

Removal of Untouchability and Social Elevation

The meanings stated as above by Dr. B.R. Ambedkar are observed in this study.

Clean Occupations

From the view-point of caste-Hindus' conception of impurity notion, commonly, the occupations which do not cause pollution to the upper caste-Hindus are considered as the clean occupations, for example; tailoring, eatables selling, carpentry, transport service and the like.

Elementary Education

The term elementary education is used to the person who is literate and whose education is upto VIII standard.

NOTES AND REFERENCES

1. Ghuge, V.B.: *Chhatrapati Shahu's Socialistic Economic Policies*, Kolhapur Zilla Parishad Publication, 1975, p. 68A.
2. Ibid., p. 97.
3. Suryawanshi, K.G.: Rajarshi Shahu: Raja Va Manus (Marathi), Thokal Prakashan, Budhwar Peth, Pune, 1984, p. 190.
4. Ghuge, V.B.: *op. cit.;* p. 101.
5. Ibid., p. 102.
6. Figures are told to the researcher on dt. 7.3.1986 by Shri S.S. Jagdale, Assistant Labour Welfare Officer, SSCSAW Mills, Kolhapur.
7. *Source*: Census of India 1981, Series 12, Maharashtra, Part II-B, Primary Census Abstract, p. 56.
8. Government of Maharashtra: Industrial Directory of Maharashtra, 1979; Pune Division, Directorate of Industries, 1981, pp. 287, 288, 291-334, and 339-350.
9. *Source*: Census of India 1981, Series-I, India, Part II B [i], Primary Census Abstract, General Population, p. 322.
10. *Source*: Census of India 1981, Series-I, India, Part II B [ii], Primary Census Abstract, Scheduled Castes, p. 220.
11. *Source*: Regional Transport Office, Kolhapur.
12. *Source*: 23rd Annual Report of Kolhapur District Cooperative Milk Producers Society Ltd., Kolhapur, p. 18.
13. Survey was undertaken by Shri P.W. Yadav, the Marketing Officer, Kolhapur District Cooperative Milk Producers Society Ltd., Kolhapur.
14. *Source:* Shri V.N. Kulkarni, Clerk of Bar Library, the Court of Kolhapur.
15. *Source:* Shri Walikhindi, C.A., Kolhapur.
16. *Source:* Shri G. Vhatkar, Architect-Engineer, Kolhapur.
17. *Source*: Dr. Sulgaonkar, Secretary, Medical Association, Kolhapur.
18. *Source:* A copy of Bankers' Clearing House dated 1.3.1986, supplied by Authority for State Bank of India, Kolhapur Main Branch.
19. *Source*: Government of Maharashtra, Vocational Survey of Kolhapur District, Education, Employment and Youth Services Department, Maharashtra, Bombay-400 032, 1980.
20. Fox, Thomas and Miller, S.M.: Art; 'Occupational Stratification and Mobility', in *Class, Status and Power*; Bendix, R. and Lipset, S.M. (ed.); Routledge and Kegan Paul Ltd., London, Reprinted 1970, p. 574.
21. Hauser and Featherman: *The Process of Stratification; Trends and Analysis*; Academic Press, New York, 1977, p. 48.
22. Ibid., p. 50.
23. Sorokin, P.A.: *Social and Cultural Mobility*, Free Press, 1964, p. 11.
24. Ibid., p. 133.

25. Abercrombie, Nicholas; Hill, Stephen and Turner, Bryan, S.: *Dictionary of Sociology;* Penguin, 1984, p. 196.
26. Tumin, Melvin M.: *Social Stratification*; Prentice-Hall, India, 1981, p. 87.
27. Ibid., p. 88.
28. Ibid., p. 89.
29. Khairmode, C.B.: Dr. Bhimrao Ramji Ambedkar Charitra (Marathi), Vol. IV, Dr. Ambedkar Education Society, Bombay-13, 1966, p. 364.
30. The Article 341(1) speaks of the power of the President; that: 'The President by public notification, specify the castes, races or tribes or parts of or groups within castes, races or tribes which shall for the purposes of this Constitution be deemed to be Scheduled Castes in relation to that State'. See, The Constitution of India, 1983, p. 178.
31. Government of India: The Constitution of India, 1983, p. 204.
32. See, Mahar, J.M. (ed.): *The Untouchables in Contemporary India*, Arizona, 1972, p. 166.
33. Kolhapur Church Council: *Western India Notes*, Vol. XLVII, April 1964, No. 2, p. 4.
34. Ibid., p. 17.
35. Khairmode, C.B.: *op. cit.;* p. 169.
36. Ibid., p. 64.
37. Good, Carter V. (ed.): *Dictionary of Education,* McGraw-Hill, 3rd edition, 1973, p. 209.
38. Ministry of Education and Social Welfare, Government of India: *Shiksha Paribhasha Kosh*, 1978, p. 45.

FOUR

A Profile of the Self-Employed Ex-Untouchables

In order to understand the mobility pattern at occupational level it is necessary to examine age, sex, caste, religion, and educational background of the respondents. In addition, phenomena like practising of modern occupations, occupational experience, intergenerational mobility and income from the source of occupation are also observed.

Personal and Social Factors

Age, sex and education towards personal, caste and religion towards social as the characteristics of the respondents are discussed below.

Age

It is generally observed that the persons belonging to the young age group give away their caste-based jobs and prefer to adopt the modern occupations. The data indicated that within the age group of below 40 years, although 18 (80%) out of 30 were still practising traditional jobs, as many as 151 out of 200 had chosen modern jobs. Thus younger people are prone to occupational mobility. With regard to older respondents it reveals that their percentage in traditional jobs is more i.e., 30, as compared to that of 22.5 per cent in modern jobs. Thus, more and more older and *older* are still *in traditional* jobs and *less in modern* jobs. The process of occupational mobility seems to have started late and as such there are a few who are above 40 years.

Sex

Out of 200 respondents only 12 were women who have adopted jobs in urban area and which are not traditional. Whereas out of 30 respondents engaged in caste-occupations, 7 women were employed by the Municipal Corporation as sweepers. Since sample covers only 6 per cent females, one cannot draw any reliable trend regarding their occupations. One of these females is Doctor and another is Tailor by profession. However, in general observation, the representation of females in the job of sweeping and other such traditional jobs appears to be more than in the modern jobs of self-employment.

TABLE 4.1: **Age brackets of 230 respondents**

Occupational category	Age Category					Total
	Between 20-30 years	Between 31-40 years	Between 41-50 years	Between 51-60 years	61 and above	
Modern occupations	87	64	35	10	4	200
Traditional occupations	10	8	7	2	3	30

Caste

The respondents selected towards the sample of the study are from the five different sub-groups of the ex-untouchable castes. The castewise distribution of the respondents is presented in Table 4.2.

TABLE 4.2: **Respondents classified by caste-group**

Occupational category	Five groups of castes					Total
	Mahar (%)	Mang (%)	Dhor (%)	Chambhar (%)	Bhangi (%)	
Modern occupations	102 (51)	62 (31)	24 (12)	8 (4)	4 (2)	200 (100)
Caste occupations	13 (43.3)	6 (20)	3 (10)	5 (16.7)	3 (10)	30 (100)
Total	115 (50)	68 (29.5)	27 (11.7)	13 (5.6)	7 (3)	230 (100)

Plate 1 : The respondent (ex-Mang) appearing in the photograph is Sales and Income Tax Practitioner.

Plate 2 : The respondent (ex-Mang), who appears in the photograph is a Laundry Proprietor.

The above table reveals that in both of the occupational categories the respondents with caste Mahars are a large in number and the Bhangis are a few. While selecting sample the castewise break-up of the respondents, of course, is not done in proportion to their populations. Hence, the sample of the respondents is approximate to the distribution of the respondents' caste. But, this representation also suggests the trend of those of Mahars and Mangs who were leading in entering into the modern occupations.

Religion

It is generally held that the ex-untouchables are Hindu by religion. The history of Hindu religion reveals the phenomenon of untouchability and hence the untouchable castes exist in the Hindu society. Moreover, there is a history of conversion also, and conversion took place mostly among the people from ex-untouchable castes. That is why, some 46 out of 230 respondents belong to other religions beside Hindu religion. Data about religion reveal that the *converted* ex-untouchables are *no longer in their caste-based* occupations and the converted 45 (22.5%) respondents represent in the modern occupational category. Taking for granted that the respondents who are converted to other religions from Hinduism, one may find that conversion and change of occupation seem to have close association. Only 1 from Buddhists was still along his caste-occupation.

Education

The educational background, especially, vocational or professional is necessary for self-employment. Generally, the persons from ex-untouchable castes do not inherit the vocational background of clean or modern occupations as persons from the groups of Gujar, Jain, Marwadi have.

The Table 4.3 reveals that those who had possessed professional or vocational knowledge were 127 (63.5%) (if category Nos. 6, 7 and 8 are clubbed) in modern occupational category. The proportion of illiterates i.e., 43.4 per cent was more among the respondents engaged in caste occupations than that of 5.5 per cent in the modern occupations. It is obvious from the table that the respondents of modern occupational category possess higher educational background than the respondents of caste occupational category. There is a growing trend among the ex-untouchables to take higher education as well as vocational training to move towards modern occupations. One may also note that as many as 95 (47.5%) respondents have remained out of vocational school, but have attained training through private practical experience and through self-learning. These are almost near to 50 per cent.

Further, if one relates caste and educational attainment in vocational or professional categories of the respondents, one comes across the following picture. In modern occupations by educational attainment Bhangi stands top (100%), Chambhar (75%), Mang (69.4%), Mahar (61.8%) and Dhor (45.9%) follow next in order. Regarding caste-based jobs the data show that the percentage of illiterates among the Mahars is the highest i.e., 53.8 per cent and in the other groups it is viz., 23.1 per cent (Mang), 15.4 per cent (Chambhar), 7.7 per cent (Dhor) and 0 per cent (Bhangi). However, these percentages are not reliable to draw any direct conclusion. Since Bhangis in this sample are only 4 in modern and 3 in caste-occupation categories, in general, one cannot draw a conclusion about the high level of education among the Bhangis. The Mahar respondents being 102 (modern) and 13 (caste), the higher illiteracy is obvious and a fact needs to be noted.

TABLE 4.3: **Educational level of the respondents**

Category of education attained		Occupational type of respondents	
		Modern occupation (%) 1	Caste occupation (%) 2
1.	Illiterate	11 (5.5)	13 (43.3)
2.	Elementary	23 (11.5)	11 (36.7)
3.	Secondary	27 (13.5)	6 (20.0)
4.	Graduate	10 (5.0)	-
5.	Post-graduate	2 (1.0)	-
6.	Professional Degree	25 (12.5)	-
7.	Vocational Course*	7 (3.5)	-
8.	Private Practical experience/self-learning	95 (47.5)	
	Total	200 (100)	30 (100)

* ITI/Radio Mechanic/Dip. in Architecture/Dip. in Agriculture/Drawing Exam.

TABLE 4.4: **Types of occupations of the respondents**

	Type of modern occupation	No. of respondents by caste group					Total
		Mahar	Mang	Dhor	Chambhar	Bhangi	
1		2	3	4	5	6	7
1	Doctor/Advocate/ Tax-consultant/ Chartered Accountant	14 (13.8)	8 (12.9)	3 (12.5)	1 (12.5)	0 (0.0)	26 (13.0)
2	Radio/Watch repairers & sellers	4 (3.9)	3 (4.9)	0 (0.0)	0 (0.0)	1 (25.0)	8 (4.0)
3	Industries owners Machinery parts stockists*	10 (9.8)	11 (17.7)	1 (4.2)	3 (37.5)	3 (75.0)	28 (14.0)
4	Transportation (goods/ passengers)	5 (4.9)	3 (4.8)	4 (16.6)	0 (0.0)	0 (0.0)	12 (6.0)
5	Publishers & Distributors/ Printer/Pen-seller/ Proprietor of Typing Institute	4 (3.9)	1 (1.7)	0 (0.0)	0 (0.0)	0 (0.0)	5 (2.5)
6	Shops of eatables	24 (23.6)	20 (32.2)	9 (37.5)	2 (25.0)	0 (0.0)	55 (27.5)
7	Cycle Mart	12 (11.8)	5 (8.00)	3 (12.5)	0 (0.0)	0 (0.0)	20 (10.0)
8	Buildings & road construction**	7 (6.8)	3 (4.9)	3 (12.5)	0 (0.0)	0 (0.0)	13 (6.5)
9	Painting	8 (7.8)	2 (3.2)	1 (4.2)	1 (12.5)	0 (0.0)	12 (6.0)
10	Tailoring	11 (10.8)	5 (8.0)	0 (0.0)	1 (12.5)	0 (0.0)	17 (8.5)
11	Other shops	3 (2.9)	1 (1.7)	0 (0.0)	0 (0.0)	0 (0.0)	4 (2.0)
	Total	102 (51.0)	62 (31.0)	24 (12.0)	8 (4.0)	4 (2.0)	200 (100)

** Mason/Plumber/Contractor/Carpenter/Architect Engineer.

* Mechanical engineering/Auto & engineering/Auto-electric/Auto motor mechanic/Manufacturing of power-loom spare parts/Lathe job-work/ Auto & Motor garage/Furniture work-shop/Secondhand machine sales and repairs/Steel fabrication/Bulldozer repairing/Oil engine repairing/ Tractor repairing/Automobile spare parts/Tyre remoulding.

Specific Occupational Categories of the Respondents

In India, in recent times, in cities a variety of modern occupations have come up and are open to any individual. Table 4.4 reveals the variation in types and percentages regarding the modern jobs with the number of persons from the different caste-groups.

The Table 4.4 indicates the trend towards the acceptance of new occupation types such as selling eatables by 27.5 per cent as the largest, followed by industrial owners and machinery stockists i.e., 14 per cent So far as the sample of this study is concerned the data suggest us that a large number of the ex-untouchables have taken up lower modern occupations and a few could take up higher modern professions. Thus the entry of ex-untouchables into modern jobs is at the margin.

If the data are examined by caste, it reveals that the Mangs (i.e., 35.5%) are leading followed by the Mahars (i.e., 27.5%) in adopting the higher modern professions (i.e., the first three occupational categories of the table 4.4). Thus so far as this sample is concerned the entry of Mangs into the self-employment jobs is suggesting a noticeable deviation from their traditional jobs.

Regarding caste-based occupations, the total sample of 30 respondents is selected according to the castewise occupational background. Thus, the respondents who inherited their caste-jobs since many generations have remained in those occupational categories which are traditional such as sweeping, playing music, rope-making and broom-making, tanning, shoe-making and scavenging.

Occupational Background

In order to understand the occupational background, the respondents' occupational experience and intergenerational occupational mobility is examined below:

Occupational Experience

There is no traditional background to the caste-groups of ex-untouchables to remain as self-employed in modern occupations. Therefore, the data concerning the respondents' occupational experience reveal the recent entry into the pattern of self-employment. The figures show that 147 respondents (i.e., 73.5%) of the total were engaged in their self-employed jobs for a period of ten years which speaks for their occupational experience. And only six respondents (i.e., 3%) have a long occupational experience for a period of 31 to 40 years. According to the figures, it is obvious that the respondents have entered into the self-employment market with just about three decades' experience.

Intergenerational Occupational Mobility

The data indicate that out of 200 respondents of modern occupation type, 14 respondents (7%) are found to have shifted from caste occupation to the modern ones and the remaining as high as 186 respondents (93%) directly took up modern occupations because of their special training. Regarding 30 respondents of traditional occupation type, it is clear that all had a background of caste-occupation. Now, let us examine the intergenerational mobility of the respondents who were engaged in modern occupations.

TABLE 4.5: **Intergenerational mobility of the respondents' fathers with their grand-fathers' occupational category**

Occupational category	Respondents' Generations	
	Fathers' generation (%)	Grand-fathers' generation (%)
1. Caste occupations	71 (35.5)	138 (69)
2. Caste-Hindus' traditional occupations*	39 (19.5)	34 (17)
3. Modern occupations	90 (45)	28 (14)
Total:	200 (100%)	200 (100%)

* Cultivating, gardening, masonry, carpentry, Zari-work, blacksmithy and stone-pieces making (Wadars').

If intergenerational occupational mobility is to be examined, Table 4.5 reveals that in comparison with the grandfathers' generation the tendency to continue the caste occupations has been decreased and in contrast, the tendency towards an adoption of modern occupations has been increased. Regarding the respondents from caste category as per their reports their previous generations pursued their caste occupations.

Thus, Table 4.5 is self-explanatory and shows clear deviation of jobs from one generation to another.

Economic Standing

While collecting the data, the income was taken into account only from that source of occupation which was considered for studying mobility aspect. The average monthly income per respondent belonging to the modern occupational type was Rs. 993.25 in the year 1984. As data reveal in the Table 4.6, as many as 125 respondents (62.5%) were receiving income ranging between Rs. 200 and 999 per month and only 33 respondents (16.5%) were receivers of income ranging between Rs. 1,500 and 5,000 per month. It shows that a majority of the respondents who received income below Rs. 1,000 per month belong to the income category of the lower middle class. But the 33 respondents, who received income more than Rs. 1,500 per month, in fact, many of them have told less than what they received and hence they belong to the upper middle class.

TABLE 4.6: **Income from occupation of 200 respondents**

Brackets of income in Rs. per month	No. of respondents in modern occupations (%)
200-499	41 (20.5)
500-999	84 (42)
1,000-1,499	42 (21)
1,500-1,999	11 (5.5)
2,000-2,499	11 (5.5)
2,500-2,999	2 (1)
3,000-3,499	4 (2)
3,500-3,999	2 (1)
4,000-5,000	3 (1.5)
Total	200 (100)

The average monthly income for the year 1985 towards per respondent belonging to the caste-jobs was Rs. 492 per month.

TABLE 4.7: **Income from caste-jobs of 30 respondents**

Brackets of income in Rs. per month	No. of respondents in caste jobs (%)
40-200	6 (20.0)
201-500	12 (40.0)
501-700	8 (26.6)
701-1,000	3 (10.0)
1,001-4,000	1 (3.3)
Total	30 (100)

Table 4.7 reveals that as many as 26 respondents (87.6%) were receivers of income ranging below Rs. 700 per month and only one was receiver of Rs. 4,000 per month. The respondent who earns around Rs. 4,000 per month is owner of a big shoe-shop in the Kolhapur city. He gets shoes made from the shoe-makers and manages trade. The other respondents except this one belonging to the caste jobs had received income just to subsist.

Thus, as compared to the respondents in caste jobs, the economic status is found to have not only changed but also raised to a higher level as the persons have taken up modern jobs.

The variation of income can be examined with the type of occupational category. The data show that only three persons belonged to the high income group i.e. Rs. 4,000 to 5,000. They were engaged in business of industrial goods and machinery, transportation and industrial jobs. The largest number i.e., 51 of the respondents seem to belong to the lower income group (i.e., below Rs. 1,000) who were engaged in jobs of selling eatables.

Regarding the Income-Tax category, the data show that out of total 230 respondents, 18 assessees were from the category of modern occupations and one was from the caste occupation (i.e., shoe-making and trading). The variation of an amount paid towards Income-Tax return is presented in Table 4.8.

The above data inform that the respondents of modern work who reached a level of Taxable Income, are more i.e., 18 (9%) than the number (3.3%) of respondents in caste jobs. Thus, the above data suggest that the adoption of modern jobs seems to be more helpful to raise one's economic status as compared to the traditional one.

TABLE 4.8: **Income-tax assessees**

	Brackets of Income-tax paid (Amount in Rs.)							Total
	25-100	101-400	401-1,000	1,001-3,000	3,001-4,000	4,001-6,000	6,001-15,000	
	1	2	3	4	5	6	7	8
No. of assessees	6	3	4	1	2	1	1	18

Native Place and Migration

As many as 188 out of 230 respondents reported Kolhapur city as their native place. The data show that the majority i.e., 159 (79.5%) of the respondents of modern occupation type have been exposed to city life since their childhood, and 35 (17.5%) of the respondents are found to be migrated from their native villages. And, the 23 respondents (i.e., 76.7%) of caste occupation type have reported Kolhapur as their native place. If the respondents' native place is examined with caste, the data show that all the Bhangi respondents of both the occupation types have a background of being brought up in Kolhapur. It is obvious for the reason that the Bhangis do not have a background of village origin especially in the Maharashtra region.

From the caste occupation type, the majority i.e., 92.3 per cent respondents among the *Mahar* group and the minority i.e., 33.3 per cent respondents among the *Mang* group have a background of Kolhapur city as their native place. From the modern occupation type, 25 per cent, 16.7 per cent, 10.7 per cent and 8 per cent respondents from the groups of Chambhar, Dhor, Mahar and Mang respectively belonged to the year bracket i.e., 41-74 category towards their life spent in Kolhapur city.

On the basis of native place as variable, it is difficult to establish the relation with the respondents' number to their mobility. Because, the data show the representation of Mahar and Mang respondents more in caste occupation type and less in modern type by its native variable.

Reasons for Migration

Table 4.9 exhibits that out of total 230, only 42 respondents have a background of leaving their villages. Out of 42 respondents, 21 have left their villages by a single reason that is; "no scope in village for their livelihood". Thus, a migration from villages is influenced by such major reason.

TABLE 4.9: **Distribution of the respondents by reason of leaving their villages**

	Category	No. of respondents (%)
1	No scope for livelihood	21 (9.1)
2	Caste obstacle to development	1 (0.4)
3	School/College education	4 (1.7)
4	Service	5 (2.1)
5	Other reasons*	9 (3.9)
6	Moved with spouse/parent	2 (0.8)
7	Not applicable**	188 (81.7)
	Total	230 (100)

* Drought, domestic quarrel, parent's death, masonry job, family dispersal and moved with son.

** Kolhapur city as permanent native place.

Summary

From the above discussion some mobility trends can be shown. After examining age group it was found that the respondents of age below 40 years were more in a number i.e., 75.5 per cent engaged in modern occupations as compared to the respondents i.e., 60 per cent in caste occupations. It indicates the association of *youngers to the modern* occupations and the *olders to their caste* occupations. Generally, it is held that women have more access in modern occupations. But in the present sample of the study, it is found that 12 women (6%) are in modern jobs as compared to 7 women (23.3%) in caste jobs. Hence, by sex, *women* are still *more* engaged *in caste jobs of sweeping* which is easier to them to supplement their family income.

According to the sample, the Mahar respondents show a large representation followed by Mang, Dhor, Chambhar and Bhangi in the modern jobs. Apart from the study-sample, the researcher has witnessed *occupational mobility among the younger Bhangis and the*

Mangs which seems to be on a par with the Mahars. Considering Kolhapur city sample, the *gap between Mahars and Mangs seems to be negligible* so far as their entry into modern occupational pattern of self-employment is concerned. The findings of occupational mobility by religion show that the converted ex-untouchables are prone to adopt modern jobs. It seems that the *conversion of religion is significant factor for occupational mobility*. The occupational mobility by education reveals that those who did not possess modern educational skill remained in their inherited caste occupations.

The data of the study reveal that a representation of the ex untouchables appears to be more in selling eatables i.e., 55 (27.5%) respondents followed by 28 (14%) respondents in industrial jobs. These figures indicate their less entry into the medium or small scale industries since the ex-untouchables do not have a rich economic background. Considering occupational experience, the data show that the ex-untouchables have entered into the modern jobs of self-employment category with an experience of about three decades which indicates for their recent beginning. In this study we have examined intergenerational occupational mobility of the respondents with their two generations of their fathers and grand-fathers. The data exhibit that every succeeding generation deviates gradually from their caste jobs and adopts the modern jobs.

Regarding economic standing respondents belonging to the *modern* occupations received Rs. 993/25 and the respondents of *caste jobs* received Rs. 492 as an average monthly income, which clearly indicates a struggle for raising one's economic status by adopting modern occupations.

The occupational mobility is also examined by the respondents' native place. By native place variable, the data relating to the occupational mobility pattern do not suit for comparison and hence difficult to derive a conclusion. But the *reason of migration from village* is reported by the respondents for their *lack of scope in their villages regarding employment and mobility access*.

In the next chapter the various sources of occupational mobility are analysed and examined in order to locate the non-economic and economic as the motivational factors.

FIVE

Occupational Mobility - The Analysis of Factors

The motivational aspect of mobility is the focus of the present study. As mentioned in theoretical framework the causes for mobility, the determinants of direction and an ambition based on self-respect notion are accounted for the explanation of motivational aspect. In the post-Independent changing situation, the number of positive and negative factors have been contributed to mobility. The background of the respondents varies by experiences, life-chances and contacts. All it influenced on their career. Such a background element is considered in the present study. Here, the motivational determinants are examined; such as encouragement by the persons in the respondents' life, the economic hardships they underwent, an ideological base, the educational qualifications, an emulation of others' actions, and the emergence of self-interest. In the light of these determinants, the occupational mobility of the ex-untouchable respondents is analysed below.

Encouragement by the Persons in the Life of the Respondents

The persons who have come in contact are not only their own family members and other kins, but also friends and other acquaintances. In an inter-personal interactions one can be influenced by others, and so some of the respondents were found to have been influenced in accepting modern occupations.

The largest number of respondents i.e., 58 (29%) from modern occupational category told that their kins/family members, friends, and sympathisers were the source of motivation for occupational mobility to them. Their guidance was found to be useful in adopting modern occupations. When the category of persons was examined, it was found that the majority of persons who guided the respondent were from the respondents' families (35). In case of 15 respondents these persons were friends and sympathisers. And in the case of 8, they were relatives who gave guidance.

After examining the type of help rendered by family members, it was found that 76.7 per cent respondents from modern occupations received monetary help and the rest of the respondents received technical assistance and encouragement. The elders of the families had introduced their sons towards the acceptance of new jobs. Further, it is worth noting that 60.2 per cent of the respondents who received help from their family members belonged to the single Mahar caste-group. The rest were from Mang (21.9%), Dhor (12.3%), Chambhar and Bhangi (2.7%). The respondents who received monetary help were those (47.9%), who belonged to either middle or lower middle class. And only 4.1 per cent belonged to the higher class. The respondents who belonged to the traditional occupational background were lacking such a family background of either financial support or consulting ability.

Thus, it is clear that monetary help is significant one and the respondents from the Mahar group were leading in receiving such help.

Economic Hardships

Generally it is held that the ex-untouchables have an inherited background of poverty. By and large, it is true. In a changing situation the traditional occupations of the ex-untouchable castes are not helpful for survival, but on the other hand a number of occupations for self-employment have become available in the present industrial and urban settings.

Therefore, in data analysis, it is found that due to the reason of economic hardships 46 respondents (23%) have adopted modern occupations and 9 respondents (30%) were stuck up to their inherited caste-work. However, those who were engaged in the modern jobs, were not so due to the motivation for shunning away their traditional jobs.

A respondent who was a banana-seller told that if he would have got a salaried job of a sweeper in the Municipal Corporation, he would have joined it for higher economic benefit. In another case, one of the 46 respondents told that as the rope-making was not profitable he had to shift towards another occupation, which was modern one. On the contrary, another respondent told that he was offered a job of sweeper but he denied to accept it as it was filthy one. The respondents (30%) from traditional occupations gave reasons for their not accepting new jobs were; poverty, unemployment, and big size of their family. Hence, they explained for their continuity in inherited caste jobs. A few of the respondents (out of 46, i.e., 23%) from modern occupations attributed their engagement in it to "supplement income".

In this way, 46 respondents got tired of economic hardships which caused to them to take up modern jobs.

When occupational background of the 46 respondents' fathers was observed, it was found that 42.8 per cent of the fathers were from the labour class category. Some 26.1 per cent of the fathers belonged to the caste-occupations. Some 19 per cent of the fathers were in the services of Class III and Class IV categories, and 11.9 per cent of the fathers carried on self-employed modern occupations. When caste category was examined, 52.3 per cent of the fathers were found from the caste-Mahar, 30.9 per cent from the caste-Mang, and 16.6 per cent from the Dhor. Thus, it reveals that the largest majority i.e., 68.9 per cent of the respondents inherited the load of their fathers' poverty and their families' adverse economic condition.

Ideological Impact

Maharashtra is the land of social reformers. Chhatrapati Shahu's upliftment policies and programmes, Dr. Ambedkar's social movements, and Karmaveer Bhaurao Patil's foundation of educational complex in the Western part of Maharashtra have influenced directly or indirectly the mental make up of the respondents. The reforms brought about by them directed and facilitated towards the career-oriented education and have helped the respondents towards the adoption of the jobs having a higher status. Apart from an ideological impact, some of the respondents became conscious of their despised status as a result of experiences and observations in their own life. Therefore, an ideological impact and the respondents' own self-awakening are taken together for the analysis purpose here.

Some 36 respondents (18%) out of 200 have told that the influence of ideologies of the reformers and the self-awakening of their own degraded status were the sources of motivation for their occupational mobility. Some 25 respondents (12.5%) out of 36, who responded towards the ideologies of the reformers can be classified further. Some 16 respondents (8%) referred to Dr. Ambedkar's call to receive education, to leave villages and to leave traditional occupations to be very effective to them.

> A respondent belonging to the Chambhar caste told that Dr. Ambedkar had come to his native village, Akol (dist. Belgaum, Karnataka State) and had appealed to the audience in order to leave their traditional jobs, as well as to abandon meet-eating of dead animals. His speech was so much inspiring and provocative that local Dalits took agitational activities and the local school was made open later on even to the pupils of all castes including ex-untouchables. As a result of it, the respondent's uncle could become the Manager of the District Industrial Centre, who further pursued his kins towards education and to the adoption of modern occupation as well.

Some 7 respondents (3.5%) told that they were attracted by Shahu's policies and programmes for the upliftment of the ex-untouchables. It can be shown from the responses of the few respondents:

> A respondent's (Dr. R.D. Pawar) father was a social worker appointed by Shahu and was made the Chairman of the Kolhapur Municipal Standing Committee. A respondent exclaimed that if Shahu Maharaj would not have brought up his father, perhaps, he himself would have been a leather-worker and never a medical doctor.

Here Shahu's indirect influence is considered as it will be seen that the fathers of the remaining 6 respondents were employed in the services of the princely Karveer State. There were 29 respondents (14.5%) whose either fathers or grand-fathers or great-grand-fathers *were appointed by Shahu* in the services of the State or who had received the benefit of Shahu's policy. They themselves had no chance of meeting or even seeing Shahu but they had guidance of their parents who were brought up by Shahu.

Some 2 respondents (1%) reported that they were encouraged by Karmaveer Bhaurao Patil himself and his educational institution, was their motivational source for receiving education.

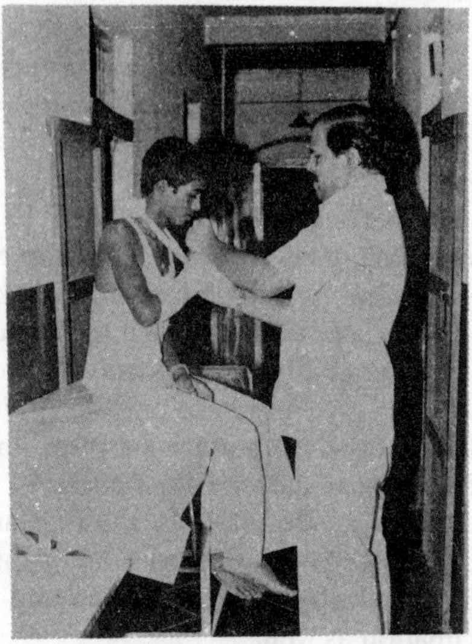

Plate 3 : The respondent (ex-Mang), an orthopaedic surgeon, is appearing as tying up a bandage to the patient in his hospital of ten cots. His motivational source is Karmaveer Bhaurao Patil.

Plate 4 : An aged respondent (ex-Bhangi) is appearing in his lathe-work-shop. In the beginning he was doing his caste-job of removing night-soil. Once he was beaten up by the upper caste-Hindus as he drank up water in a glass in the hotel. The moment enlightened him to deviate from his caste-job, and initially he worked as a cleaner in a Christian's motor work-shop.

A respondent, Dr. S K. Ghate (Mang) told that he could become an orthopaedic surgeon because he was provided all types of facilities and support during his school-days as he was admitted to the learning centre started by Karmaveer Bhaurao Patil. If not, he might have remained as a drum-beater (one of the major activities of Mang). Another, who got educated in Karmaveer's school was also influenced by a slogan of 'self-dependence'.

Another ideological element regarding 'the self-awakening of the respondents, which is revealed by the 11 respondents out of 36 as their motivational source of their occupational mobility. In what way the respondents became self-conscious of their filthy work can be judged from a few of the responses.

A respondent belonging to the Dhor caste-group realized himself that due to his tanning activities he had observed a difficulty in interactions with the upper caste-Hindu fellows. Another respondent of the same group revealed a similar type of experience. A respondent from the Mang caste-group also revealed his realization of his caste-work as stigmatised. Moreover, a respondent from the Bhangi group revealed his experience that some upper caste-Hindus had treated him badly. Once he entered a Sodawater shop and drank water up for which he was severely beaten. From the very day of an inciden he realized of his night-soil removing job and swored to abandon it, and joined as a cleaner in motor workshop. Now he is independently managing lathe machines. Another Bhangi respondent also realised his work as stigmatised.

While classifying the ideological influence by caste, it was found that the Mahar respondents (21) were the largest in a number; followed by that of Mang (7), Chambhar (3), Dhor (3) and Bhangi (2). If it is examined among its caste population, the Bhangi respondents appear to be leading i.e., 50 per cent followed by Chambhar (37.5%), and Mahar (20.5%), Dhor (12.5%), and Mang (11.2%) as the *lowest* in its ideological influence. Of course, the sample of caste is not representative one.

The above discussion is explained with regard to the 200 respondents of modern occupations. But such ideological influence is found to be absent among those respondents who were engaged still in their inherited caste-work.

Educational Qualifications

By virtue of the Constitutional provisions and the post-independent compensatory or protective policies and programmes of the Government, the members of the scheduled castes population motivated towards the education. The professions such as medical practice, legal practice, tax-consultancy, chartered-accountancy and the like require a professional degree or a diploma course to enter into such professions. The members of the scheduled castes could get educational opportunities because of the post-matric scholarship and the reservation facilities. How educational qualifications led the scheduled castes members directly towards an accepting modern occupations can be seen from the following discussion.

The data reveal that the educational qualifications directly influenced upon the 26 respondents (i.e., 13%) to adopt the esteemed professions. Those respondents were doctors, advocates, tax-consultants, chartered-accountant, radio-watch repairers and businessmen. Here, it is necessary to mention that in spite of the respondents' professional qualifications or vocational training or experience, all have not told their educational qualifications as their motivational source of occupational mobility. Therefore, educational qualifications (degree/diploma/training/experience/knowledge) is not regarded as the principal motivational source but rather it is viewed by the respondents as secondary one.

However, the importance of educational attainment was proved to be helpful as the means for occupational mobility. That is why, as many as 117 respondents (58.5%) told in the context of another question that they could prepare well for their modern occupations as they had an educational background. Thus, 'education' has certainly proved as the significant factor for occupational mobility.

Emulation of Others' Jobs

Some 19 respondents (9.5%) adopted modern jobs by emulation. Most of them have emulated the work of their previous employers. The respondents' previous employers were the proprietors of steel industries, motor vehicle body builders, and plumbing and building contractors. Five respondents were such who emulated the occupations of their friends. A few of them have adopted the jobs of their neighbour and relative. This emulation again can be explained along with their previous experience in such jobs. Such a matter of experience or opportunity in modern jobs does not reveal in case of the respondents from the jobs of traditional category.

Arousal of Self-Interest in Particular Jobs

Some 8 respondents (4%) adopted modern jobs because of their own interest in the particular jobs. Some four respondents adopted as their self-interest in an independent occupation and 2 respondents in tailoring, and transportation service, and the remaining 2 in radio repairing through trial and error practice. Here also, a job experience factor is in the background for their self-interest.

Other Sources

Lastly, some 7 respondents (3.5%) were exposed to their different sources of their mobility. Four out of 7 respondents were exposed to the city characteristics like occupational freedom and the emergence of secular attitude of the urban dwellers. Remaining 1 out of 3 respondents was motivated towards the medical service to the poor and the other 2 respondents were exposed to the means of communications, i.e., both had read the advertisement of training course in a local daily newspaper (i.e., *Pudhari*) which ultimately found them to be useful in adopting the modern jobs. Thus, in the case of those 3 respondents, the development of impersonal life of city and the occupational training seems to be instrumental to them in taking up modern jobs.

Discussion

Considering the independent variables, occupational mobility is analysed according to the different sources of motivations, i.e., (i) an encouragement by the persons in the background, (ii) the economic hardships, (iii) an ideological impact, and the educational qualifications. These have contributed to the ex-untouchables' occupational mobility. Although, these motivational sources are attributed to their occupational mobility, these cannot be taken into account as the sole factors.

There are other factors such as financial assistance rendered by the institutional agencies and the service opportunities given by the Christian Missionaries in their Institutes to the respondents' parents. Moreover, the post-Independent Constitutional measures and the special legislation in favour of the members of scheduled castes have raised their morale and encouraged them in taking up modern jobs. Considering these special institutional measures and programmes of the Government, occupational mobility certainly shows to be a syndrome of both 'the subjective' and 'the objective' attributes.

A number of financing agencies are set up by the Government to render the loan-facility for the capital investment. The MPBCDC is the principal financing agency to provide financial assistance to the members of the Scheduled Castes. Also, an access to either professional or vocational institutions for the training and experience of occupational knowledge and skill enabled the persons of weaker sections towards the higher level of education. A system of representation to the scheduled castes members in the public bodies like Municipal Corporation vis-a-vis the roles of social reformers in bringing about social transformations in liberalizing the attitudes of the high caste-Hindus created an atmosphere congenial for progress in the different fields. Consequently, a leadership from the group of SCs got developed, and it further kept the process of upliftment into gear. These objective conditions facilitated the members of Scheduled Castes to prepare and aspire for taking up modern jobs. Thus, a manifestation of the desire to come up and the subjective conditions of the respondents, are the outcomes of the above mentioned objective conditions. Let us examine how far other determinants also appear to be instrumental in contributing occupational mobility.

Financing Institutions

The Table 5.1 reveals that as many as 101 respondents are rendered financial assistance by the different agencies. But again it indicates that the Nationalised/the Cooperative Banks and the MPBCDC agencies seem to be the *major in rendering the financial assistance*. Moreover, it is informed by the Manager of one of the Nationalized Banks that such financial assistance for self-employment is rendered as a matter of 20-Point Programme of the Government. It means, as many as *50 per cent* of the respondents could get advantage due to the *Government's policy* of helping the persons belonging to the weaker sections.

TABLE 5.1: **Financial assistance rendered by the Financing Agencies**

Category of Financing Agency	No.of respondents assisted
1. Nationalized/Cooperative Banks	57 (28.5)
2. Mahatma Phule Backward Class Development Corporation	28 (14)
3. Financing Corporations (MSFC/ MSSIDC/WMDC)*	3 (1.5)
4. District Industrial Centre	2 (1)
5. Private Sources (father/relative/ friend/money-lender)	10 (5)
6. Sanjaya Gandhi Niradhar Yojana	1 (0.5)
Total	101 (50.5)

* Maharashtra State Finance Corporation/Maharashtra Small Scale Industrial Development Corporation/Western Maharashtra Development Corporation.

Government's Educational Policy Towards the Scheduled Castes

The significance of educational attainment for the development of occupational skill is instrumental for taking up of modern jobs. As data show that as many as 117 respondents could get prepared for the modern occupations due to their professional and vocational background. Some 28 out of 117 respondents were such who received the benefit of government's policy of reservation and post-matric scholarship during their educational career. As a result of such policy 28 respondents could become the professionals as Doctors, Advocates, Tax-consultant, Chartered Accountant and Architect Engineer.

Reservation of Political Seats in the Public Bodies

By virtue of the Constitution of India, the members of the Scheduled Castes get opportunity as representatives in the Municipal Corporation. Three members from the Mang caste-group have a background as the representatives in the Kolhapur Municipal Corporation. As a result of their local power political connections some 7 respondents

Plate 5 : The respondent (ex.Mang) is appearing in the photograph - at the receiving counter of his hotel. He is an elected ex-corporator in the local municipal council.

Plate 6 : The furniture proprietor is a converted-Christian known for his origin as ex-Mahar.

from the Mang caste-group got advantage of getting an accommodation for their modern occupational activities.

Service Opportunities in the Christian Missionaries' Institutions

In Kolhapur and its region, a complex of educational, medical and evangelistic institutions and agricultural and industrial works is set up and developed by the Christian Missionaries (please see Appendix-V). In such Missionaries' Institutions many of the ex-untouchables had received the benefit of service opportunities. As a result, some 27 respondents who had a background of being Christian by religion, were engaged in the present modern jobs. These respondents' parental generation was benefitted by the Christian Missionaries either in the form of service or other jobs. Thus, the role of Christian Missionaries was strong backing to those 27 respondents. On the other hand, one can find from the present data that not a single respondent from the converted-Christian was engaged in the hereditary nature of caste-occupations. Thus, one may say that 'change of religion' and change of occupation are going together so far as this sample is concerned.

Conclusion

Thus, occupational mobility of ex-untouchables can be explained as a syndrome of both subjective and objective determinants. The motivational sources, *viz.*, (i) encouragement by the persons in the background, (ii) economic hardships, (iii) ideological impact, and (iv) the respondents' educational qualifications can be taken into account as the subjective determinants for occupational mobility. Second, the policy of protective discrimination in favour of Scheduled Castes groups adopted by the Government of India, and the Maharashtra Government as well, *viz.*, (i) assistance to weaker sections for self-employment under the Twenty-Point Programme, (ii) reservation and post-matric scholarship to the students of scheduled castes, (iii) reservation of seats in the public bodies to the members of scheduled castes; and in the historical background, the job opportunities given by Shahu Chhatrapati in his State and also by the Christian Missionaries to the ex-untouchable persons can be taken into account as the objective determinants of mobility.

In the next chapter, an attempt is made to show whether the respondents have achieved success in their adopted modern jobs. On their success or failure it may be decided whether social mobility has been resulted because of change in occupation; in other words, whether change of occupation can be taken as instrumental in bringing about social mobility.

SIX

Occupational Mobility - Its Success and Consequences

In the Chapter 'Theoretical Framework', the ageold traditional notion of pure-impure opposition as the root of occupational and social immobility of ex-untouchables is already discussed. Now-a-days, in the post-Independent India since modern industrial-urban pattern and open normative system are developed, the notional sense of pure-impure opposition is presumed to be weakened and also presumed to be given way to the occupational mobility, and in consequence a social mobility.

In this chapter, the discussion focusses on the occupational success, the adoption of modern occupations causing wider social interactions and the continuity by respondents' children in their occupations. To measure occupational success, the satisfaction of the respondents in their self-employment, the caste-category of customers and the awareness of the respondents' castes by their customers and in consequence their continuity to remain as customers too, are considered here. In addition to these indicators, the perception of the respondents themselves towards their own specification in adopting jobs, is also taken into account to assess the success.

Secondly, an attempt has been made to assess the degree of adoption of modern occupations and perception of the respondents in raising their own status in society. Lastly, an attempt has been made to assess the occupational aspirations of the respondents about their children as to whether they aspire for upper occupational choice. Now, let us examine the success and the consequences of occupational mobility in detail.

Occupational Success

Here, the following aspects are discussed for measuring the occupational success:

Occupational Experience

The reaction of the respondents towards their job-satisfaction is considered as one of the indicators of occupational success. Out of 200, as many as 176 (88%) and 24 (12%) respondents engaged in modern jobs have expressed either their satisfaction or partial satisfaction respectively towards their jobs adopted. No body expressed dissatisfaction.

On the basis of the data a broad division of modern occupations is made into the satisfaction and the partial satisfaction in the adopted jobs of the respondents. It is shown in the Chart given below:

CHART I: Division of jobs based on the respondents' information towards their jobs satisfaction

Jobs in which respondents reported 'satisfaction'	Jobs in which respondents reported 'partial satisfaction'
1	2
1. Vegetable selling, dairy, flour mill, chilly and masala pounding machine, grains shop, Pan shop, fruits selling, tea and Bhaji stall, egg-omelet stall, hotel, tea canteen, ice-cream sales service, soda-water shop, fire-wood selling, grocery shop	1. Groundnuts and grams selling 2. Auto-electric service 3. Truck transport 4. Legal practice 5. Tyre-remoulding and sales
2. Medical practice, Tax-consultancy, Chartered Accountancy, Architect Engineering	
3. Tailoring, laundry service	
4. Cycle-mart shop, watch and radio repairing and sales service, selling of lottery tickets	
5. Motor and auto-garage, body-building	

of auto, jeep and truck, auto and engineering industries, foundry, lathe-work-shop, machine mechanical engineering, tractor repairing, mechanical workshop, tempo-transportation, manufacturing of power-loom spare parts, furniture workshop and sales, sound service, auto-rickshaw carriage, steel works, steel fabrication, steel fabrication of agricultural implements, motorcycle mechanic, scooter and auto-rickshaw mechanic, automobile spare-parts sales, and machine job work

6. Hand and spray colouring, commercial and building paintings, paints and hardware shop

7. Building contractor, masonry, plumbing and carpentry

8. Books publisher and distributor, printing, typing institute, pen, lighter and torch selling

---

The respondents who reported their explanation towards partial satisfaction are given in brief below:

1. The respondents who were engaged in a job of groundnut and grams selling reported their dissatisfaction for the only reason that such economic activity gives income just to subsist.
2. A respondent engaged in Auto-Electric service job reported his partial satisfaction because of the location of his job, is the locality of prostitutes (Dombarwada). And all other respondents engaged in such a job of auto-electric service reported that, it is seasonal one and so it is slack in rainy season. Hence, it limits their earning.

The respondent, an Advocate (ex-Mahar), whose economic background is rich.

3. A respondent who chose truck transport service reported his disappointment over his job for the loss that he had to bear due to the occurrence of an accident.[1]
4. Two of the respondents of Advocate profession told their partial satisfaction due to their recent entry into legal practice.[2]

Especially, regarding the modern and the self-employed jobs, generally, it is said that there is no guarantee of continuity in such jobs. Considering a *mean period of 27.6 years* for 200 respondents' occupational experience in modern jobs, such assumption does not hold true. Hence, the satisfaction expressed by all respondents engaged in modern jobs, can be taken as a good indicator so far as their occupational success is concerned.

Caste-Category of the Customers

As many as 191 (95.5%) out of 200 respondents of modern jobs told that their customers mostly belonged to the society at large and not only from their own castes or even closer to their castes. A dairy owner respondent, whose service of milk distribution is home delivery and who is Mahar by caste reported that most of his customers were from the Brahmin caste. Another respondent, whose profession is Sales and Income-Tax Consultancy, and who belongs to Mang caste told that his customers were mostly from the upper castes, *viz.*, Gujar, Jain and Maratha. It seems that customers including upper caste-Hindus have not been particular in selecting salesmen. This factor of *customers' broad and open choice* also contributes to their occupational success.

Knowing of Caste and Remaining as Consumers

Out of 200, as many as 96 (i.e., 48%) respondents reported that their customers were knowing their castes. Despite the knowledge of the respondents' castes, customers remained as customers. However, as low as 13 (6.5%) respondents reported that a few of their customers discontinued as a result of lowest caste-origin. Even then, this seems to be an encouraging feature, so far as begetting confidence on the part of self-employed respondents engaged in modern jobs is concerned.

Reason of Success as Stated by the Respondents

The above two indicators reflect the view of customers. Here, the respondents' perception of specification of reason of occupational success is examined. As many as 175 (87.5%) respondents out of 200 have singled out 'the performance'[3] as the reason of their occupational success.

The respondents explained their performance in a variety of ways which could be observed in their occupational activities. The performance can be classified at three levels, *viz.*, personal conduct, behaviour towards others and the services rendered to their customers. Their performance at personal conduct level could be judged from their being away from unhealthy habits of smoking and drinking (of course those who observed they explained). Many of them told that they were away from the habits of drinking and smoking. By behaviour towards customers and others meant by them is an avoidance of quarrel, a respectful behaviour in public and cordial interaction with others. Thus, they tried to maintain mutual cooperation with customers. By services they meant paying it sincerely whenever required, proper maintenance and repairing of cycles, proper management, sometimes providing credit facility, weighing proper weight of the goods, reasonable rates, selling of unadulterated goods, serving of quality tea, maintenance of cleanliness, medical services in low rates as compared to others, guarantee of service, satisfactory services, keeping dried firewood for sale, a mechanic's average speciality of two-three wheeler vehicles, to be in the shops during the open-hours, and the like.

Consequences of Occupational Mobility

In this present study, social mobility is considered as a consequence of occupational mobility of ex-untouchables. It is so considered, because, in traditional India the general conception of pollution was attached to the members of the ex-untouchable-groups since their engagement in filthy occupational jobs.[4] Their engagement in such jobs was regarded ritually polluting and hence their lowest social status was determined by it. This has been discussed at length in the first chapter, 'Theoretical Framework'. Further, how these changes are brought about in the present time is elaborated with recent examples in the same chapter.

In the following discussion, I have examined whether the respondents have got over their pollution-barrier by adopting modern occupations or not. So, in this study social mobility is confined to interactional levels such as commensal and friendship for measurement purpose. The hypothesis: 'Persons' adoption of occupations which are not regarded as contemptuous removes the stigma of untouchability; and such persons become acceptable to the upper caste-Hindus for social interactions'; is tested in this study. Here, social mobility is measured at the levels of ego and family. Let us see whether occupational mobility or other factors are perceived by the respondents as instrumental in raising their status in society.

Ego Level

As many as 196 (98%) respondents of modern jobs category and some 17 (56.7%) of caste jobs category perceived themselves elevated of their status in society. The respondents' perception is examined at different interactional levels. Table 6.1 reveals that majority of the respondents from the category of modern jobs category reported positive response towards their interaction with upper caste-Hindu fellows. Two of the interactional experiences revealed by the respondents are mentioned below:

1. A Bulldozer and Oil Engine repairer respondent (Mang) told that most of his friends from all upper caste-Hindus come to his residence especially for non-vegetarian food.
2. A respondent (Mahar) of 79 year old, a social worker and a staunch follower of Dr. Babasaheb Ambedkar told that Ghatage and Patil, the well-known industrialists in Kolhapur attended the wedding ceremony of his son and took meal at his home place.

The interactions at consultation level also reported that upper caste-Hindu fellows consulted 115 respondents (57.5%) for either opinion or advice about socio-personal and economic matters. A respondent (Mahar), an owner of the paints and hardware shop expressed that his relations are so developed with a *Marwadi* family that for any valuable or other purchase like clothes and other articles he is consulted and taken to purchase. Hence, it is evident from Table 6.2 that upper caste-Hindus regard ex-untouchable persons in various socio-economic activities to be on par and consider them worthy of consulting on important matters. This speaks of the rise in the social status of ex-untouchables because of their experiences in new occupations.

TABLE 6.1: **Reported Interactions by the Respondents (200) of Modern Jobs Category**

Category of Interactions	Number of Respondents (200)		
	Yes	No	Not applicable (%)
1	2	3	4
1. Interdrinking of tea and other liquids	189 (94.5)	7 (3.5)	4 (2.0)
2. Interdining	186 (93.0)	9 (4.5)	5 (2.5)
3. Distance not observed in personal relations	196 (98.0)	–	4 (2.0)
4. Got rented house of high caste-Hindus	25 (12.5)	–	175 (87.5)
5. Got plot and constructed house in the locality of high caste-Hindus	31 (15.5)	2 (1.0)	167 (83.5)
6. Invited by the high caste-Hindu friends/colleagues/neighbours for marriage, religious ceremony	193 (96.5)	2 (1.0)	5 (2.5)
7. When invited by the respondents, the high caste-Hindu friends/ colleagues/neighbours come to home for marriage and other ceremonies etc.	190 (95.0)	6 (3.0)	4 (2.0)
8. Got accommodation for occupation	49 (24.5)	1 (0.5)	150 (75.0)

TABLE 6.2: **Number of Respondents who were Consulted by Upper Caste-Hindus**

	Items	Number of Respondents Out of 200
1	Organising any public programme	15
2	Establishing educational institution	10
3	Appointing a member on public body	10
4	Promoting a cooperative society	12
5	Purchase of a plot/house construction/ light connection, and the like	19
6	Starting of a business or other economic activity	19
7	Choosing a marital partner	10
8	Purchase of clothes/vehicle	9
9	Guidance in choosing educational career/ course	4
10	Any other (i.e., association-formation, raising funds for public purpose, family problems, bank loans, well digging and food serving in marriage)	20

For comparison, the responses of the respondents of caste jobs were examined. Some 17 respondents (56.7%) perceived themselves elevated of their status in spite of their engagement in filthy jobs. To the question regarding the type of relations with upper caste-Hindu fellows, the data report that 19 respondents (63.3%) had equalitarian relations, 6 (20%) had discriminatory and 5 (16.7%) had no interactions with upper caste-Hindu fellows. Further, the form of discrimination inquired and 6 (20%) respondents reported that discrimination was observed by pouring water from a distance and also by *using a separate plastic glass or a glass-vessel for drinking water* to them. A female respondent responded that sometime she was addressed as *'Maharni'*, a caste utterance of the upper caste-Hindu persons when she was doing her sweeping job. However, a few of the sample in spite of the respondents' engagement in their filthy jobs, Table 6.3 reveals the inter-actions of ex-untouchable members with upper caste-Hindu fellows. A shoe-repairer respondent expressed that a friend from *Maratha* caste attended his wedding ceremony but *left without taking* a meal. In another case, some Maratha friends took meal on wedding occasion at tanner's home. Especially, three Bhangi respondents revealed that in spite of their engagement in the scavenging job, some friends from *Gujar, Brah-*

min and Maratha castes not only attended the wedding and the other ceremonies but took meal as well at their dwelling places.

TABLE 6.3: **Reported Interactions by the Respondents (30) with Upper Caste-Hindu Fellows**

Items of Interactions	Yes (%)	No (%)	Not applicable (%)
1 Interdrinking of tea and other liquids	21 (70)	—	9 (30)
2 Interdining	16 (53.3)	4 (13.3)	10 (33.3)
3 Distance not observed in personal relations	19 (63.3)	2 (6.7)	9 (30.0)
4 Invited by upper caste-Hindus for marriage, religious ceremony, and the like	16 (53.3)	3 (10.0)	11 (36.7)
5 When invited, upper caste-Hindus come to the respondents' home for marriage and other ceremonies	13 (43.3)	4 (13.3)	13 (43.4)

The above data reveal that the respondents of both occupational types perceived an elevation of their status. And, as many as 173 (86.5%) respondents of modern jobs category attributed *adoption of modern occupation* as the major contributing factor, and *educational development* and *personal conduct* as its secondary towards their status elevation. Whereas, some 4 (13.3%) respondents of their caste jobs attributed *clean living, urban secularism* and *changing attitude of upper caste-Hindu fellows* towards their acceptance for commensal and friendship relationship.

After examining a comparative data, it reveals that the respondents of modern jobs category who perceived their status as elevated are more i.e., 196 (98%) to 17 (56.7%) of caste job respondents, however, a few sample. At the level of interaction and consultation, data show that some discrimination was observed against the persons engaged in their own caste occupations. However, the respondents of modern jobs category attributed 'adoption of modern occupations' towards their status raising. Thus, it can be stated that it is contributing element to the elevation of the social status of those of ex-untouchables.

Family Level

If one's individual status changes, it affects the status of the family. Therefore, the status of the respondents' families was considered in the study. Hence, it is examined in its consideration towards the direct consequence of occupational mobility.

As many as 165 (82.5%) respondents of modern jobs category perceived their members of the families that they are looked upon, and 16 (53.3%) respondents of caste jobs perceived their members of the families that they are not looked down as dirt as in the past. Here, the respondents' perception towards their families is examined at different interactional levels of commensality and friendship with the upper caste-Hindus.

TABLE 6.4: **Interactions of the members of the Respondents' (200) families with the upper Caste-Hindu Families**

Category of interactions	Number of Respondents		
	Yes (%)	No (%)	Not applicable (%)
1 Going for shopping together	122 (61)	44 (22)	34 (17)
2 Showing new purchases	136 (68)	30 (15)	34 (17)
3 Exchange of new saris/ ornaments for wearing	60 (30)	106 (53)	34 (17)
4 Inviting for preparation of homemade food products	95 (47.5)	71 (35.5)	34 (17)
5 Interdrinking and exchange of cooked food	158 (79)	8 (4)	34 (17)
6 Playing of children together	127 (63.5)	23 (11.5)	50 (25)
7 Inviting for marriage, naming ceremony, haldikunku, puja, etc.	157 (78.5)	9 (4.5)	34 (17)
8 Inviting for preparation of food at wedding engagement, marriage, birthday, diwali-festival and the like	80 (40)	86 (43)	34 (17)

Above Table 6.4 manifests itself for the interactional relationships of the members of the respondents' families with the members of the upper caste-Hindu families. A doctor-respondent (Mahar) revealed that once his wife was called for by a *Marwadi* family for making chapatis. In another case, in spite of the respondent's ordinary job of vegetable selling, she was invited by a Maratha family to make chapatis.

For comparison, let us examine the type of interactions of the members of the respondents' (of caste jobs) families with those of the upper caste-Hindu families. The data reveal that a good number of respondents' families i.e., 18 (60%) had equal relationship with the members of the upper caste-Hindu families. In the case of three respondents I was told that a few poor Maratha families lived in the locality of ex-untouchable groups, and they had interactions at commensal level with those of ex-untouchable families. A shoe-shop owner also told that his family relations were extended at commensal level with those families of Jain, Brahmin and Maratha castes.

TABLE 6.5: **Interactions of the Members of the Respondents' (30) families with the upper caste-Hindu-families**

Category of interactions	Number of Respondents		
	Yes (%)	No (%)	Not applicable (%)
1 Going for shopping together	13 (43.3)	4 (13.3)	13 (43.3)
2 Showing new purchases	13 (43.3)	3 (10.0)	14 (46.7)
3 Exchange of new saries/ ornaments for wearing	6 (20.0)	9 (30.0)	15 (50.0)
4 Inviting for preparation of homemade food products	10 (33.0)	5 (16.7)	15 (50.0)
5 Interdrinking of tea and exchange of cooked food	15 (50.0)	2 (6.7)	13 (43.3)
6 Playing of children together	13 (43.3)	4 (13.3)	13 (43.3)
7 Inviting for wedding, birthday, puja, haldikunku, and the like	15 (50.0)	2 (6.7)	13 (43.3)
8 Inviting for preparation of food on wedding engagement, marriage, birthday, diwali festival and the like	9 (30.0)	6 (20.0)	15 (50.0)

Again, it cannot be overlooked that 10 (33.3%) respondents' families, who confined their relationship with their own caste fellows. Table 6.5 obviously indicates that about half of the respondents' families have not extended their relationship outside their own caste fellows. A few of them had, and reported that they had limited relationship at tea-drinking level with the members of the Maratha, the upper caste-Hindus. But, in spite of the scavenging job of Bhangis, all the three respondents told of their interrelationship that they had at the level of *commensal and friendship with those of Brahmin and Maratha families*.

After examining Tables 6.4 and 6.5, a comparative data exhibit that the persons who have become free from their filthy jobs and adopted modern jobs are acceptable to the upper caste-Hindus for interactions. Secondly, the persons who are in their caste jobs hesitate to develop interactions with the upper caste-Hindus due to their age-old inferiority complex, and moreover, such persons are exclusively identified as ex-untouchables by the upper caste-Hindu persons.

With regard to the respondents' (of modern jobs) family level interactions, here again as many as 105 (52.5%) respondents attributed 'adoption of modern occupation' and 28 (14%) respondents attributed 'rising standard of living' for the irinteractions with upper caste-Hindus. Whereas, 14 (46.7%) and 11 (36.7%) of the respondents (of caste jobs) have attributed 'income', and 'clean living and good behaviour' respectively for their interactions with the upper caste-Hindus. The majority of respondents of both modern and caste jobs reported their interactions which took place especially with the fellows from Maratha, and in spite of a numerical minority, the next are from Brahmin and Jain castes. Moreover, as many as 144 (72%) respondents of modern jobs reported to have no experience of interactional discrimination during these recent changing times. Thus, the persons who have adopted modern jobs are found to have developed their interactions with the upper caste-Hindus on equal footings.

Occupational Aspiration of the Respondents Against their Children

How far the respondents' jobs would be succeeded, is examined through the respondents' perception about occupational aspirations against their children. The object of studying such aspirations is due to the lack of occupational background of self-employment to the ex-untouchable persons, and as a result of respondents' experience whether they wanted their children to be prevented from self-employed jobs or to be continued in it.

It is told that in Kolhapur City, the hotel was opened to the ex-untouchable people for the first time on dt. 5-11-1945. The photograph of opening ceremony appears.

Seating members from right: Adv. Tendulkar, the then Municipal President, Adv. R.T. Bagade, Gangaram Kamble, a social worker, Narayanrao, the hotel owner, and Bhai Madhavrao Bagal.

When the respondents' aspiration was examined, 66 respondents of modern jobs reported their positive aspirations towards their own self-employed jobs. Although 61 respondents reported negatively, 44 respondents reported it for the reason that their children should attain higher education, and join any other more status-giving occupation. A majority of the remaining 17 respondents indicated their refusal because they have seen their occupations which give income just to subsist. Those occupations are auto-rickshaw carriage, fruits selling, flour mill service and the like.

Whereas, 7 (23.3%) respondents of the caste jobs were found to be prone to put their children in their own caste jobs. Six (20%) respondents have already put their children in their caste jobs. The respondents who have shown their positive response to put their children in caste jobs, majority of them are from *Mahar, Mang and Bhangi* castes. These respondents were working *as sweeper in the Municipal Corporation*. They perceived a job of sweeper as secured employment for their children. A few respondents were from *Chambhar and Dhor* castes who also *perceived security of employment in their leather and tanning activities*. Some 17 respondents (of caste jobs) who reported negatively, some 9 of them have reported for the reason that their children should attain higher education.

Thus, from the above data, as compared to the respondents of caste jobs, the respondents of modern jobs are more aspirants for their children's better occupational mobility.

Summary

The above discussion is focussed on success achieved by deviating from caste jobs and adopting the modern ones. The social mobility at ego and family levels is also examined towards it. The occupational aspiration of the respondents with regard to their children is also examined.

The occupational success is measured at three levels *viz.*, (i) occupational experience, (ii) the caste category of the customers, and (iii) despite the knowledge of caste whether customers remained as customers. In addition, from the view-point of the respondents also, the reasons of their success are examined. I have found that nearly all respondents doing modern jobs expressed satisfaction. Secondly, as many as 95.5 per cent respondents reported satisfactory acceptance from the upper caste-Hindus. Some of the respondents gave credit to their own *performance*.

In this present study, social mobility is measured in its interactional relationships with the upper caste-Hindus towards the consequence of occupational mobility. At ego level, as many as 196 (98%) and some 17 (56.7%) respondents from modern and caste jobs respectively perceived their status as elevated as they could have their commensal and friendship interactions with the upper caste-Hindu fellows. At family level also, as many as 165 (82.5%) and some 16 (53.3%) respondents from modern and caste jobs respectively perceived of their status as elevated. The comparative difference between these figures of the two different job categories clearly indicates the consequence towards social mobility.

Regarding occupational aspirations of the respondents with regard to their children, the findings of the data show that the persons at modern occupational level have high aspirations and whereas, some persons of caste jobs have put their children in their jobs for the additional source of income. Thus, it obviously indicates that the higher aspires for still higher than the lower ones.

NOTES AND REFERENCES

1. At the moment of interview, respondent's truck was not usable for transportation service.
2. One Advocate who reported his satisfaction has a very good background of his economic standing. He did his LL.B. at Pune. He got trained under the guidance of the senior Advocate for some months at Pune. After his professional training and experience, he started his independent practice at Kolhapur. He has set his office with modern furniture and attractive library. He used to attend his office and the court sometime either by his Ambassador car or by his motor cycle. Also, he possesses a good knowledge of his profession.
3. Meaning of Performance: 'Performance presupposes standards of correctness. It applies to what are considered to be legitimate means or to the good which must conform to standards of correctness as well as of efficiency. If an action has been performed it must sense to ask whether it was done correctly, skillfully, and so on.' - Peter, R.S.: *The Concept of Motivation*, Routledge and Kegan Paul, London, 1958, p. 115.
4. The traditional jobs of the five groups of the present study were and now, however, all on the wane; *viz.*, 1. Mahars' removing of cattle carcasses, village watchmanship, as a village messenger and village servant, and food habits of carrion eating. 2. Mangs' drumming of leather instruments, midwifery, and making of rope, basket and broom. 3. Chambhars' curing hides and preparing shoes. 4. Dhors' tanning, i.e., making saddles and water-bags, cutting and drying skins. 5. Bhangis' removing of night-soil and sweeping.

SEVEN

Major Findings, Conclusions and Suggestions

This chapter presents major findings which are discussed in the previous chapters and which were about different aspects of occupational mobility observed among the ex-untouchable castes persons from the area under study.

Major Findings

The major findings are offered below:

Within the age group of below 40 years, 18 (60%) out of 30 respondents were still practising traditional jobs and 151 (75.5%) out of 200 respondents of the same age group had chosen modern jobs. Some 49 (24.5%) persons between 41 and above were engaged in modern jobs, while 12 (40%) of the same age group were in the traditional jobs. This finding indicates positive association between young age and modern jobs. Of course, those who could not shift to modern jobs earlier are naturally older in age.

Out of 200 respondents, 12 (6%) women were found engaged in modern jobs, 7 (23.3%) out of 30 respondents were still working as sweepers, and 10 out of 12 women were doing the job of selling eatables. Thus, women are earning their livelihood but following old routine type job. Parmar's study of Surat sample reveals the similar trend of females' entry into the vegetables and fruit selling jobs.[1]

Although the respondents selected from their respective caste-groups are not in proportion to their population figures, still one can understand the trend by the information collected. The *Chambhars in my sample are less prone to adopt modern* occupations than other caste persons and they have remained engaged in their leather activities as these have scope even in these changing times.

Occupational mobility has been found to be the characteristic feature among the converted ex-untouchables more prominently than among the Hindus.

The respondents who possess modern education, professional or vocational skill have found easier to do modern jobs and those who remained still deprived of education or have remained less educated have to do even today their old jobs.

The data by occupational category show the trend towards an acceptance of occupation such as selling eatables by 27.5 per cent respondents which is the largest, followed by 14 per cent in the jobs of Industries and Machinery Stockists, and by 13 per cent in the professions like Medical, Legal, Tax and Accountancy Practice. Such findings about occupational entry of the ex-untouchable persons indicate for their emerging trend of entrepreneurship in modern jobs. It is true that entry into such occupations is not considerable. A study based on Poona City sample undertaken by Patwardhan before a decade and a half noted that in spite of industrialization only a few occupations at the lower end of the occupational hierarchy had been opened to the lowest caste groups.[2] Now, by the recent finding of the present study, it is evident that ex-untouchable persons are coming forward so as to gain an advantage of the changing times and are entering the jobs of middle occupational categories of the modern professional market.

The largest entry of Dhor respondents were 37.5 per cent, and it is found in the occupational category of selling eatables; Bhangis 75 per cent in the industrial jobs category and Mahars 13.7 per cent in the professional category such as medical practice, legal practice and the like.

Regarding income received from that source of occupation which was reported by the respondents in this study, data revealed that an average income per respondent belonging to the modern occupations was Rs. 993.25 per month in 1984, as compared to that of respondents doing caste jobs it was only Rs. 492 per month in 1985. It is obvious that modern job is the source of high income.

The majority (60.2%) of respondents, who received monetary or technical help and encouragement from their family members, belonged mostly to the Mahar caste-group. Further, it was found that as high as *95.8 per cent Mahar respondents had a background of middle class culture*.

The Mahar respondents (21) who seem to have influence of reformers' ideas are the largest in a number. It clearly indicates that *Mahars are exposed to the movements led by the reformers*.

Plate 8 : The spectacled respondent (ex-Bhangi), who has adopted radio-repairing as his occupation, appears in the photograph.

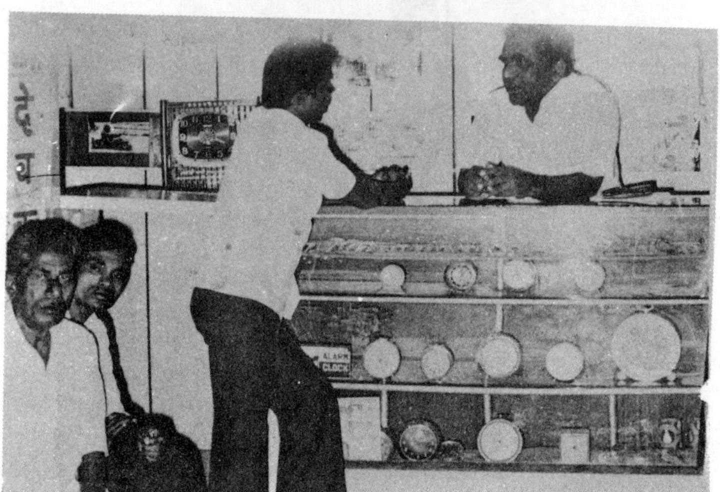

Plate 9 : The respondent (ex-Mang) appearing in the photograph motivated some of his kins to take up watch-repairing job by giving them training and experience opportunity in his own shop. He got elected as a Corporator in the local Municipal Council.

Plate 10 : A tea-bhaji stall of the respondent (ex-Mang)

Plate 11 : The respondent (ex-Mahar), who appears in the photograph, is managing his dairy, and distributies milk to his customers at their home-places also. Most of his customers belong to the group of upper caste-Hindus. Some of his customers are also aware of his caste.

Plate 12 : The owner of the motor-body-building workshop avoided to appear in the photograph as he was afraid of losing some customers and some tenders. He revealed such experience in some cases when his caste (ex-Chambhar) was brought to the notice of others.

On an average, the respondents have an *experience of 27.6 years in their modern occupational careers*. This fact reveals for the recent deviation of the sons' generation from their parents' age-old caste jobs.

No respondent engaged in modern occupations expressed dissatisfaction about his occupational experience. Out of 200 as many as 191 respondents had customers from all the castes and not only from their own or other ex-untouchable castes. Except on a rare occasion they had discriminatory experience from one or two customers.

As many as 175 out of 200 respondents of modern jobs have singled out the factor of '*their performance*' responsible for their occupational success.

The majority of respondents of both jobs categories reported of their commensal and friendly interactions with the upper caste-Hindu fellows, but 6 (20%) and 5 (16%) respondents of caste jobs reported discriminatory treatment and no interactions respectively with upper caste-Hindu fellows. The majority of respondents of both modern and caste jobs reported of their interactions which usually take place especially with the fellows from Maratha, Brahmin and Jain castes in its sequential order. Thus, one finds effective mingling and inter-action between caste-Hindus and ex-untouchable respondents so far as their business, economic exchanges and customer-provider relationships are concerned. It indicates that caste barrier hardly comes in the way of occupational mobility among these groups.

Regarding occupational aspirations of the respondents against their children, the data revealed that the persons who are in modern jobs have high aspirations as compared to those of doing caste jobs.

Conclusions

Some of the important conclusions are stated below:

Out of 200, some 58 respondents (29%) who adopted modern jobs did get guidance and help in financial and technical matters from the elder members of their families, relatives, friends, and sympathisers. On the other hand, the respondents of caste jobs could have neither family background of such guidance nor of financial support. Thus a family background found to be as one of the contributing factors for mobility.

Some 46 respondents (23%) who have taken up modern jobs, by family and socio-economic background, were suffering from economic hardships caused by their inherited caste works, poverty, unemployment, and more depending members of their families. Thus the unfavourable background caused them to move from their traditional way of living.

Among the respondents who have accepted modern jobs, some 25 respondents have witnessed the change in their behaviour and decision making due to the reformists' ideologies. Some (11) got awakened from their down-trodden state of life and only because of it they could accept new jobs. Some (18) were motivated by reformers' ideology, and also by friends' and kins' guidance. These awakening, reformists' and liberal ideologies as well as strong egalitarian motivation are behind the social change among these downtrodden sections who could realize their motivation into practice by changing occupation. Thus, occupational mobility is not only an economic but a socio-economic phenomenon. As a result, the role of reformers' ideologies found to be effective in deviating from the tradition way of life.

The educational qualifications of 26 respondents (13%) directly influenced to adopt the esteemed professions such as medical practice, legal practice, tax-consultancy, and the like. On the other hand, the respondents of caste jobs lacked educational attainment to enter into the modern occupational market. Emulation of modern jobs practised by friends, neighbours and relatives caused occupational mobility in case of 19 (i.e., 9.5%) respondents. Thus the Constitutional measures proved to be instrumental to occur mobility among the Scheduled castes.

Some 8 respondents (4%) through self-interest created by job-experience have taken up the jobs of tailoring, transportation service and radio-repairing.

Financial assistance rendered by the Mahatma Phule Backward Class Development Corporation, Kolhapur, the Nationalized and the Cooperative Banks under Government's 20-Point Programme of raising economic status of the poor was *found to be instrumental to 83 respondents* (42.5%) of the modern jobs.

Those who have benefitted as a result of Government's Constitutional commitment, although a few, have utilized many educational and other facilities provided to them.

Similarly, *47 respondents* (23.5%) who have a background of *Christian religion*, have been benefitted by the Christian Missionaries' welfare services.

Regarding social elevation of status, as high as 86.5 per cent respondents of modern jobs attributed to 'adoption of modern occupations' as the major factor, and educational development and personal conduct as secondary factor towards their commensal and friendship interactional relationships with the caste-Hindu fellows. On the other hand, 4 respondents of caste jobs (however very few) have attributed *'clean living'*, *'urban secularism'* and *'changing attitude of caste-Hindus'* for their interactions. In short, the socio-economic changes brought about in the life of those of scheduled castes people can be ascribed to the modern values developed in contemporary India.

To conclude that; without the historical and post-Independence background of protective discrimination policies and programmes, the mobility of ex-untouchables into the modern jobs, perhaps, would have been difficult.

Suggestions

The author is aware of limited validity of the findings in view of a short sample of 230 respondents. However, a few suggestions could be made in order to strengthen the findings of this study, from further research point of view:

(1) Similar studies, if conducted in different developing cities, would enable to gain knowledge about factors other than those revealed in the present study.

(2) Groups of ex-untouchables in different places could be observed not only on interactional level but also on levels like class, class position, neighbourhood, selection of mates for marriage, day-to-day rituals as well as religious behaviour.

(3) "Ex-untouchables' changing traditional occupations and their interaction with Maratha community" in urban and rural contexts at one point of time can be studied in order to assess the impact of modern values and attitudinal change in two societies.

(4) At the practical level, I want to make the following suggestions to the respective administrative authorities at local as well as States levels:

(a) Present provisions of financial assistance need be strengthened so that more ex-untouchable persons can be benefitted.
(b) Seminars, workshops and other counselling services should be provided to the young engineers, technicians and entrepreneurs from time to time.
(c) In case wherever and whenever there is construction for market by the Local Administrative Authority, some parts of it should be made available to the members of the Scheduled Castes by making a provision on the principle of reservation.
(d) In order to seek the place in the self-employment market, the persons (from ex-untouchable group), who came up as entrepreneurs, technicians, engineers, legislators, government officers and social activists should come forward to provide some counselling services regarding the sources of financial assistance, accommodation, marketing requirement, and the like to the deserving persons from the deprived groups.
(e) State Governments should set up the Entrepreneurship Development Institute for Scheduled Castes and Scheduled Tribes to develop their skill to start the industry, and managerial and marketing skills also.
(f) Government should adopt a policy of licenses to be issued in preference to the entrepreneurs belonging to SC/ST.

NOTES AND REFERENCES

1. Parmar, Y.A.: 'Occupational Variation in Scheduled Caste of Surat: A Case of Mahyavanshi' in *South Gujarat University Journal,* Vol. X, 1981, pp. 9-20.
2. Patwardhan, Sunanda: *Change Among India's Harijans*, Orient Longman, 1973, pp. 203-4.

APPENDIX-I

Occupational Mobility among the Persons from Ex-untouchable Castes in Kolhapur City

INTERVIEW SCHEDULE-I and II

Section-I

1. Name:

2. Present residential address (Locality):
   i) Homogenous
   ii) Mixed

3. Age:
   i) 20-30
   ii) 31-40
   iii) 41-50
   iv) 51-60
   v) 60 and above

4. Sex:
   i) Male
   ii) Female

5. Marital status:
   i) Married
   ii) Unmarried
   iii) Widow
   iv) Widower

6. Do you have children?
   i) Yes
   ii) No
   iii) Not applicable

7. Caste:
   i) Mahar
   ii) Mang
   iii) Dhor
   iv) Chambhar
   v) Bhangi

8. Religion:
   i) Hindu
   ii) Christian
   iii) Buddhism
   iv) Islam

9. Educational Qualifications:
   i) Illiterate
   ii) Elementary
   iii) Secondary
   iv) Graduation
   v) Post-graduation
   vi) Professional degree
   vii) Vocational course: ITI/Radio Mechanic/Dip. in Architecture/Dip. in Agriculture/Drawing examination
   viii) Private practical experience/self learning

10. Present occupational activity:
   i) Doctor/Lawyer/Tax-consultant/Chartered Accountant
   ii) Radio/Watch repairer and seller
   iii) Industrial and Machinery Parts stockists: Mechanical engineering/Auto and engineering/Auto-electric/Auto and motor machanic / Manufacturing of power-loom spare parts / Lathe job-work / Auto and motor garage / Furniture work-shop / Secondhand machine sales and repairs / Steel fabrication / Bulldozer repairing / Oil engine repairing / Tractor repairing / Automobile spare parts / Tyre remoulding
   iv) Transportation: Truck / Tempo / Autorickshaw
   v) Books-publisher and distributor / Printer / Pen-seller/ Typist

vi) Shops of eatables:
Fruits / Vegetables / Tea and Bhaji / Grocery / Canteen / Ice-cream / Pan-shop / Soda water / Dairy / Groundnut and gram selling / Egg-Omlete / Flour mill and chilly pounding machine

vii) Cycle mart

viii) Building and road construction:
Mason / Plumber / Contractor / Carpenter / Architect Engineer

ix) Painters:
Commercial / Building / Spray

x) Tailoring

xi) Other shops:
Paints / Firewood / Lottery / Laundry

11. Since how long in present occupation:
   i) 3 months-04 years
   ii) 05-10 years
   iii) 11-20 years
   iv) 21-30 years
   v) 31-40 years

12. Location of occupation:
   i) Market centre
   ii) Residential locality
   iii) Non-specific place

13.1 Monthly Income from present occupation:
   i) Rs. 200-499
   ii) Rs. 500-999
   iii) Rs. 1,000-1,499
   iv) Rs. 1,500-1,999
   v) Rs. 2,000-2,499
   vi) Rs. 2,500-2,999
   vii) Rs. 3,000-3,999
   viii) Rs. 4,000-5,000

13.2 Are you Income Tax payer?
   i) Yes
   ii) No

13.3 If yes, what amount you paid previous year?

i) Rs. 25-100
ii) Rs. 101-400
iii) Rs. 401-1,000
iv) Rs. 1,001-3,000
v) Rs. 3,001-4,000
vi) Rs. 4,001-6,000
vii) Rs. 6,001-15,000

Section-II

1. What is the occupation of the following kins and relatives?

i) Father's
ii) Mother's
iii) Grand-father's
iv) Great-grand father's
v) Elder brother's
vi) Husband's

Section-III

1. What is your permanent native place?

i) Kolhapur
ii) Other city
iii) Town
iv) Village (District...)

2. Since how long are you here in Kolhapur?

i) Years 01-10
ii) Years 11-20
iii) Years 21-30
iv) Years 31-40
v) Years 41-50
vi) Years 51-74

3.1 If you are from a village, why did you leave it?

i) No scope for economic survival
ii) Caste an obstacle for development
iii) School/college education
iv) Service

v) Any other (credit uneconomical, domestic quarrel, drought, parent's death, masonry activity, becoming poor, family dispersal)
vi) Not applicable (moved along with spouse/parent)

3.2 Who migrated first to Kolhapur from the following:
i) Respondent
ii) Elder brother
iii) Father
iv) Grand-father/mother/great-grand-father
v) Husband
vi) Husband's father / Husband's great-grand-father
vii) Any other (uncle/great grand-mother)
viii) Not applicable

3.3 If yes, what is the reason for migration?
i) Livelihood
ii) Service / search of service
iii) Rule of caste
iv) Education
v) Adopting independent occupation
vi) Any other (plague / hospital service to kin / drought / poverty / transfer)
vii) Not applicable

Section-IV

1. Did you follow your caste-occupation?
i) Yes
ii) No

2. Why did you take up new occupation?
i) Felt stigmatized
ii) Not profitable / loss in occupation
iii) Industrial encroachment
iv) Educational qualifications / vocational training or experience
v) Change in career
vi) Source of self-employment / subsistence
vii) More investment not required

viii) Available through succession
ix) Any other (interest in occupation, low education, physically handicapped, supplementary income, shortage of capital)
x) Not applicable

3. How could you prepare for present occupation?
i) Educational qualification / vocational knowledge / training / experience / self-learning / self-enlightenment
ii) Succession of non-traditional occupation
iii) Self-employment as source for livelihood
iv) Encouragement and support of relatives / friends and availability of government facility

4.1 Have you taken any financial aid for the investment in occupation?
i) Yes
ii) No
iii) Not applicable (in case where more capital not required)

4.2 If yes, who financed from the following:
i) Nationalized / Cooperative Bank
ii) Mahatma Phule Backward Class Development Corporation
iii) Financing Corporation (MSFC, MSSIDC, WMDC)
iv) District Industrial Centre
v) Private Source: Friends / Money-lender / Father / Relative
vi) Any other (Employment office / Sanjaya Gandhi Niradhar Yojana)
vii) Not applicable

4.3 How did you enter into the present occupation?
i) On own efforts
ii) Through the help of a political leader / District Industrial Officer / Relative
iii) Through personal contact
iv) Through succession / spouse / patrimonial kin

Section-V

1. What is the source of motivation from the following?
   i) Impact of Shahu's upliftment and developmental policies for untouchables and others
   ii) Dr. Ambedkar's call to receive education, to leave villages, to leave traditional occupations, etc., and his conversion of religion
   iii) Availability of loan facility (MPBCDC / FC, Bank, etc.)
   iv) Kin's / friend's / other's suggestion / guidance encouragement / persuasion
   v) Arousal of self-interest
   vi) Educational opportunities / vocational knowledge / self-awakening (i.e., caste activity stigmatised / self-respected activity)
   vii) Emulation of other's activity
   viii) Economic survival
   ix) Any other (service to poor, occupational freedom in city, independent feeling, advertisement reading)

Section-VI

1.1 Whether any other member from your family has been instrumental in beginning the present occupation?
   i) Yes
   ii) No

1.2 If yes, specify the member(s)
   i) Parents / great-parent
   ii) Patrimonial kin
   iii) Matrimonial kin
   iv) Any other (spouse, son, brother-in-law)

1.3 Mention the type of help rendered by kin:
   i) Monetary
   ii) Technical
   iii) Consultancy
   iv) Introducing others
   v) Encouragement / assistance in work

vi) Availability of activity through succession
vii) Not applicable

2.1 Who possessed the ownership of land from the following?
i) Parent
ii) Patrimonial relative
iii) Spouse / spouse's kin

2.2 If yes, type and area of land:

(a) Irrigated:
i) Below 02 acres
ii) 02-05 acres
iii) 06-10 acres
iv) 11-50 acres

(b) Unirrigated:
i) Below 02 acres
ii) 02-05 acres
iii) 06-10 acres
iv) 11-31 acres

3.1 Who left agricultural occupation?
i) Respondent
ii) Father
iii) Other kin / spouse
iv) Not applicable

3.2 Reason for abandoning agricultural occupation:
i) Financial insecurity
ii) Lack of cooperation by the villagers
iii) Possession of mortgaged land by money-lender / land taken away under tenancy act
iv) Cultivation of waste and small holding of land as uneconomic
v) Quarrel among brothers
vi) Adoption of modern occupation
vii) City attraction for occupational scope
viii) Not applicable

Section-VII

1. What is your reaction about your present occupation?
   i) Fully satisfied
   ii) Partially satisfied
   iii) Fully dissatisfied

2. Who are your customers / clients ?
   i) From own caste
   ii) From other castes and closer to own caste
   iii) From society at large

3. Whether your customers have knowledge of your caste?
   i) Many
   ii) Few
   iii) None
   iv) Not applicable

4. When the customers become aware of your caste, how many of them discontinued?
   i) Nobody
   ii) Few
   iii) Many
   iv) Not applicable

Section-VIII

1. What helped from the following to become successful in your occupation?
   i) Performance
   ii) Conversion of religion to Christianity
   iii) Change in surname
   iv) Concealed caste identity / not identified
   v) Most of the customers from own caste and closer to caste
   vi) Changing attitude of upper caste-Hindu members
   vii) Source of father's activity
   viii) Personal relationship

Section-IX

Whether a changeover from the traditional occupation to the present one was instrumental in raising your status from the following viewpoints:

From Ego's Viewpoint:

1. Do you find yourself elevated in status from what you were?
   i) Yes
   ii) No
   iii) Cannot say (relations confined to own caste brethren)

2. If caste-Hindu colleagues / friends / neighbours are aware of your caste, specify the type of interactions from the following:
   i) Interdrinking
   ii) Interdining
   iii) Distance not observed in personal relations
   iv) Got rented house of a upper caste-Hindu
   v) Got plot and constructed house in the locality of a upper caste-Hindus
   vi) Invited by an upper caste-Hindu friends / colleagues / neighbours for marriage, religious ceremony, etc.
   vii) When invited, upper caste-Hindu friends / colleagues/ neighbours come to your home for marriage and other ceremony, etc.
   viii) Got accommodation for occupation
   ix) Not applicable

3.1 Whether you are consulted for opinion or inquiry or advice by an upper caste-Hindu person about the secular and other activities?
   i) Yes
   ii) No
   ii) Not applicable

3.2 If yes, mention the following:
   i) Organising any public programme
   ii) Establishing educational institution
   iii) Appointing a member on public body

iv) Initiating a cooperative society
v) Plot purchase / house construction / light connection
vi) Initiation of business or any activity
vii) Choosing marital partner
viii) Cloth / vehicle buying
ix) Educational / career / course guidance
x) Any other (i.e., formation of an association, raising funds for public activity, family problems, bank loan, type of food to be served in marriage, well digging, etc.)

4. What helped in elevation of your status from the following:
   i) Adoption of modern occupation
   ii) Educational or intellectual development
   iii) Education and income
   iv) Standard of living
   v) Personal conduct
   vi) Personal contacts with the influential upper caste-Hindu persons
   vii) Important position occupied by a relative
   viii) Interrelationship developed at student stage
   ix) Social service in Court, Office, Bank matters, etc.
   x) Associational activities
   xi) Not applicable

From Family's Viewpoint

1.1 Whether the members of your family are looked upon as socially advanced?
   i) Yes
   ii) No
   iii) Cannot say (in case of relations confined to own caste members)
   iv) Not applicable (in case of respondent if alone)

1.2 What are the interactions of your family members with the upper caste-Hindu neighbours' / friends' family members from the following:
   i) Going for shopping together
   ii) Showing new purchases

iii) Exchanging new saris/ornaments for wearing
iv) Inviting for homemade products
v) Interdrinking / exchanging of cooked food, etc.
vi) Playing of children together
vii) Inviting for marriage, birth, prayer, haldi-kunku, etc.
viii) Inviting for the preparation of food occasionally at wedding engagement, marriage, birth, diwali festival, etc.
ix) Not applicable

2. What helped in elevation of your family status from the following:
   i) Adoption of modern occupation
   ii) Rise in standard of living
   iii) Family members' relationship with upper caste-Hindu fellows
   iv) Change of residence
   v) Respondent / kin relative is social / political worker
   vi) Maintaining cordial relations with others
   vii) Education of family members
   viii) Friendship at student stage
   ix) Any other (i.e., intercaste marriage, helping nature, political work)
   x) Not applicable

Section-X

1.1 Whether you like to engage your children in your present occupation?
   i) Yes
   ii) No
   iii) Not thought over
   iv) Choice left to children

1.2 If not why?
   i) Children should join other prestigious or service occupation
   ii) Children be highly educated
   iii) Occupation has rare scope in future (e.g., secondhand machine repairs and sales)

iv) Present occupation low-income giving
v) Any other (i.e., daughter cannot do a pan-shop job)

2.1 Whether your children like to continue your present occupation?
i) Yes
ii) No
iii) Not applicable (if already joined other activity, in case of under-age)

2.2 If yes, why?
i) Occupation well regarded
ii) Occupation can be continued without caste observation
iii) Occupation profitable / subsistence giving
iv) Occupation unfilthy
v) Be continued as occupation of father / already activity available
vi) Contacts are extended with various caste fellows and thereby high regard can be achieved
vii) Interest in activity
viii) Independent activity

2.3 If children do not like to continue, why?
i) Liking towards more prestigious occupation
ii) Liking towards service occupation
iii) Any other (i.e., doctor has to oblige at any hour of a day or night, low profit)

INTERVIEW SCHEDULE-II

Section-I

1. Name:
2. Present residential address:
3. Age:
   i) 20-30 years

ii) 31-40 years
iii) 41-50 years
iv) 51-60 years
v) 61 and above

4. Sex:
   i) Male
   ii) Female

5. Marital status:
   i) Married
   ii) Unmarried
   iii) Widow
   iv) Widower

6. Do you have children?
   i) Yes
   ii) No
   iii) Not applicable

7. Caste:
   i) Mahar
   ii) Mang
   iii) Dhor
   iv) Chambhar
   v) Bhangi

8. Religion:
   i) Hindu
   ii) Christian
   iii) Buddhism
   iv) Islam

9. Educational qualification:
   i) Illiterate
   ii) Elementary
   iii) Secondary

10. Present occupation:
   i) Sweeper / crematory service
   ii) Leather musician / Rope or Broom maker

iii) Tanner
iv) Shoe-maker
v) Scavenger / Night-soil remover / Drainage clearer

11. Monthly income from above activity:
i) Rs. 040-200
ii) Rs. 201-500
iii) Rs. 501-700
iv) Rs. 700-1,000
v) Rs. 1,001-4,000

Section-II

1. What it is your permanent native place?
i) Kolhapur
ii) Other city
iii) Town
iv) Village (Dist.....)

2. If you are from a village, why did you leave it?
i) No sufficient scope for livelihood
ii) Un-economic land
iii) Any other
iv) Not applicable

Section-III

1. Why do you follow the traditional occupation?
i) Passed down from parent
ii) Helpful in survival
iii) Profitable
iv) Lack of modern education
v) No alternative source of employment
vi) Any other

2. How did you enter into the present occupation?
i) Self willing
ii) Parental instruction

3. What is your reaction about your present occupation?
   - i) Satisfied
   - ii) Dissatisfied
   - iii) Insulted

Section-IV

1.1 Who possessed the ownership of land from the following?
   - i) Respondent
   - ii) Father
   - iii) Not applicable (if landless)

1.2 If yes, type and area of land:
   - i) Irrigated
   - ii) Unirrigated
   - iii) Not applicable

Section-V

Whether the traditional activity is instrumental in raising your status in the changing modern situation from the following viewpoints:

From Ego's Viewpoint

1.1 Now, do you find yourself elevated in status?
   - i) Yes
   - ii) No
   - iii) Cannot say

1.2 What are the types of relations with the upper caste-Hindus?
   - i) Equalitarian
   - ii) Discriminatory
   - iii) Avoidance by the upper caste-Hindu fellows
   - iv) No interaction with upper caste-Hindu fellows

1.3 If you are discriminated, what is the nature of observation of it?
   - i) Physical distance
   - ii) Drinking in a separate pot / pouring from distance

iii) Dining at separate seat
iv) Not applicable

1.4 If not discriminated, what are the interactions with the upper caste-Hindus from the following:
i) Interdrinking of tea and other liquids
ii) Interdining
iii) Distance not observed in personal relations
iv) Invited by upper caste-Hindus for marriages, religious ceremony, etc.
v) When invited upper caste-Hindus come to your home for marriage and other ceremonies

1.5 What do you attribute to raise your status?
i) Income
ii) Clean living
iii) Urban secularism
iv) Changing attitude of caste-Hindu fellows
v) Unable to answer

From Family's Viewpoint

1.1 Whether the members of your family are looked down as dirty or socially backward?
i) Yes
ii) No
iii) Cannot say
iv) Not applicable

1.2 What are the types of interactions of your family members with the upper caste-Hindus?

i) Equalitarian
ii) Discriminatory
iii) Avoidance by the caste-Hindu fellows
iv) Not applicable

1.3 If not discriminated, what are the interactions of your family members with the caste-Hindus from the following?
i) Going for shopping together

ii) Showing new purchases
iii) Exchanging new sari/ornament for formal wearing
iv) Inviting for preparation of homemade products
v) Interdrinking and exchanging of cooked food
vi) Playing of children together
vii) Inviting for ceremonies such as marriage, birth, prayer, haldi-kunku, etc.
viii) Inviting for the preparation of food for ceremony such as wedding engagement, marriage, birth, diwali festival, etc.
ix) Not applicable (in case of relations not extended outside of caste brethren)

1.4 What do you attribute to raise your family status?
i) Income
ii) Clean living and good behaviour
iii) Children's education and their modern occupation
iv) Urban secularism
v) Changing attitude of caste-Hindu members
vi) Unable to answer
vii) Not applicable

Section-VI

1.1 With regard to your children's vocation, do you like to engage your children in your present traditional occupation?
i) Yes
ii) No
iii) Not thought over
iv) Choice left to children
v) Not applicable

1.2 Whether your son/daughter is engaged in caste jobs?
i) Yes
ii) No
iii) Not applicable

1.3 If not, why?
i) Children be educated

ii) Children should join other prestigious or service occupation
iii) Under age
iv) Low-income giving job
v) Job stigmatized
vi) Not applicable

1.4 If yes, Why?
i) It is subsistence giving
ii) It is lucrative
iii) Security of employment
iv) Not high educated
v) Parent's job be continued
vi) Not applicable

APPENDIX II

Role of the Reformers

Account of the upliftment of untouchables and the removal of untouchability will never be complete and realistic if the names and work of Jotirao Phule, V.R. Shinde, Shahu Chhatrapati and Dr. Babasaheb Ambedkar are not given due coverage. The centres of their activities were mainly the different parts of Maharashtra region. In order to attain the objectives, these reformers had introduced different programmes and strategies such as educating downtrodden people for their self-improvement, attaining political power to redress the grievances, representations and agitations for reformatory legislations, and action programmes for exercising their rights. Modern legislation is also adopted as important instruments for bringing about reformatory changes in the traditional normative structure. They succeeded in many of their programmes with the support of British Government's liberal policy in matters of caste-disabilities, practices engendered by religion and age-old traditions. Legislation also worked as powerful instrument to bring about certain changes in the established patterns of Hindu society.

The efforts of social reformers broadly influenced in two ways. First, it influenced modern legislation leading to an end of old customary practices. And secondly, their action programmes influenced in changing the attitudes of caste-Hindus towards the ex-untouchables. Whatever the progress of ex-untouchables in different fields of education, politics, economic and social has taken place, is the outcome of social reformers' efforts. These reforms have been effective in liberating downtrodden communities from caste-restrictions.

Post-Independent discrimination and reformatory legislation in the interests of the scheduled caste people, and in general, the people of India have a long history of continuous struggle. Most of the reformers who struggled are from Maharashtra. During the end of nineteenth century, first Jotirao Phule demanded recruitment in the government services to all castes people in proportion to their population.[1] On similar lines of Phule, in 1917 Chhatrapati Shahu demanded special caste-based representation for non-Brahmins including the ex-untouchables to the Montagu-Chelmsford Commission and it was granted. In 1919 written statements were submitted by Dr. B.R. Ambedkar, G.A. Gavai, V.R. Shinde, B.V. Jadhav and others to the Southborough Committee for the communal representation of the depressed classes in the Legislative Council. They were called and examined. It granted few seats. In 1917, a resolution of removing all disabilities upon depressed classes was passed in the Calcutta annual meeting by the efforts of V.R. Shinde, and in 1920 in the Nagpur Congress annual meeting, Mahatma Gandhi succeeded in admitting a subject of removal of untouchability as a part of Congress Manifesto. Later on, credit goes to Mahatma Gandhi for making a programme of removal of untouchability and the issues of ex-untouchables as a part of Congress Party activities. In 1928, Dr. Ambedkar submitted a statement to the Indian Statutory (Simon) Commission for the protection of depressed classes through special and adequate representation in the Council and he was called for evidence before Simon Commission. On the recommendations by the Indian Franchise (Lothian) Committee, Dr. Ambedkar as a delegate represented the Round Table Conference in 1931-32 held in London for the representation of depressed classes in the future Constitution. On 16th August, 1932 the Communal Award was issued granting separate electorates for the depressed classes. But Dr. Ambedkar had to withdraw the Award due to Mahatma Gandhi's fast unto death and heavy pressure from caste-Hindu leaders and historically known as Poona Pact signed on agreement made on the 25th September, 1932 by providing 148 reserved seats for depressed classes. For republic India, Dr. Ambedkar being the Chairman of the Constituent Assembly and chief architect of the Constitution of Independent India did his best to protect the interests of the Scheduled Castes and the Scheduled Tribes as well. Thus, the roots of compensatory discrimination policy through special legislation can be traced out in the historical struggle of social reformers.

THE ROYAL REFORMER - SHAHU CHHATRAPATI

Role of Shahu Chhatrapati

Social Condition of Untouchable Castes

Till the accession of Shahu Chhatrapati to the throne, the state of social condition in Kolhapur State of Maratha country was predominated by the rule of Brahmanism. For example, a ritual practice of distributing sweet-meat was observed on specific day (Gurudwadasi) at Nrisinha Wadi under the supervision of the Mamlatdar (Magistrate) of Shirol sub-division in Kolhapur State. Till 1907 sweet-meat was distributed only among the Brahmins, and for receiving it the Brahmin Mamlatdar had disqualified all other non-Brahmins. When Khanderao Bagal, belonging to the Maratha caste was appointed in place of Brahmin Mamlatdar, for the first time, he had started distributing sweet-meat down to the ex-untouchables. The similar practice was stopped by him at Samangad. When the intermediate castes such as Maratha and others had to suffer from the caste-disability, it is obvious of ex-untouchables for their worse state. Latthe, the biographer of Shahu Chhatrapati described the state of ex-untouchable classes in Kolhapur State during the rule of Shahu. He described: 'Untouchables had to live outside the village. They were not to draw water from the public well. They were not to enjoy the benefits of the public rest-houses. They could not touch the water of the tank or pond of the village. They were not to enter the household of the caste-Hindu. The land which a family held was not to give a living for a week in the year, one had to obey the order of the village officer to run to the Taluka town, which was away thirty or forty miles to deliver the post. One had to be ready for the service of the Police or Revenue Officer whenever he had visited. He had to run after the horse of a officer. All it was in return for a piece of land. In many cases untouchable boys were not admitted to the school classes. In case, admitted, he had to sit outside the class room'.[2] Thus, the ex-untouchables were ostracised from the ordinary rights of man.

Ways of Liberation

In the background of closed hierarchical order of Brahminism, especially to liberate the ex-untouchables, Shahu Chhatrapati adopted radicalism at different levels. First, he adopted a way of practising himself. In matters of reformation he was of the view that the persons who desire reformations, first they should take lead in initiating reformatory actions. Mahatma Phule had started movement of education for girls and he began from his wife by educating her, and he had opened his cistern to the untouchables of time. Similarly, Shahu Maharaj followed to practice first. He legalised all inter-caste marriages among Hindus and Jains and took initiative to advise Maharaja Holker of Indore who belonged to Dhangar caste, lower to Maratha for inter-caste marriage between the Yuvaraj (prince) of Indore and daughter of the Junior Chief of Kagal, a kin to Shahu Maharaj. In a letter of Jan. 16, 1920 written to Maharaj Holkar for his intended interdining and intercaste marriages, Shahu explained: 'If poor relatives contract such marriages, they will be outcasted. I work among the untouchables and the masses... others naturally follow me'.[3] At the occasion of All India Maratha Education Congress held on dt. 27.12.1917 at Khamgaon, Chhatrapati said in his presidential address; "it is the responsibility of the upper caste people to take lead in the movement of all reformations as higher Samurai warrior class in Japan had taken in breaking down their traditional restrictions." Thus, he was motivated towards reformations. Secondly, he introduced reformation through legislation in matters of social, education, etc. He did not stop over passing the legislation, but he was vigilant and careful of execution of his orders by appointing non-Brahmins to important posts and by accompanying men from the poor classes.

The role of Shahu relating to ex-untouchables can be classified into- (i) creating educational opportunities, (ii) providing service opportunities in the State, (iii) inducing towards self-employment jobs, and (iv) removing of disabilities of caste and untouchability through legislation, its execution and encouragement towards the possession of political power, etc. What Shahu has made revolutionary changes at different levels especially to liberate the ex-untouchables, is outlined below:

Educational Programmes

Shahu Chhatrapati adopted educational programmes for depressed classes at the levels of school, hostel, and training for service and independent profession. The social reality of the caste system of the time was that the people of high caste were not ready to allow their ward to sit along with other lower caste boys in the class-room. So in the beginning Chhatrapati had to open separate schools for each caste to induce the boys from backward and depressed classes. Later on by order No. 340 of dt. 30.9.1919 Chhatrapati stopped such practice of separate schools and opened admission for other castes, and banned the practice of untouchability in the schools. It is reported that during 1907-08, there were 16 schools for ex-untouchable boys in the Karveer State. Chhatrapati adopted a policy of hostel accommodation for girls also from the depressed classes and for that the applications were invited.

To facilitate education, Shahu Maharaj took initiative in opening hostel for the depressed classes boys. The hostel opened for them was named after Miss Clarke, the daughter of the then Governor of Bombay. Miss Clarke was taking interest in the cause of ex-untouchables. D.S. Powar, the then Chairman of Standing Committee of Kolhapur Municipality and ex-M.L.A. was the student of the same hostel. Considering the caste distinction among the groups of ex-untouchable castes, Maharaj had opened separate hostel for the Dhor-Chambhar boys too.

To encourage the students from the depressed classes, Shahu granted freeship in fee and scholarship. And by order of dt. 25.6.1919 Chhatrapati extended scholarship facilities to the trainee of talathi (village revenue officer) from an ex-untouchable caste. As a result of Shahu's policy and programmes the strength of ex-untouchable students which was 234 in 1894 increased to 2,162 in 1921-22.

Shahu did not satisfy on general education. He extended his programme to professional education and training to the persons from depressed classes to create self-confidence of being equal to other individuals of upper caste-Hindus. Moreover, he explained his objective that the professions which were closed to the depressed classes due to customs and religious laws should be made open for the elevation of their status. Shahu selected Ganacharya (Mang), Mandpalkar (Mahar), Ramu Karande and D.S. Powar (Chamar) for the education of lawyer. After completion of their education, the Sanads (certificates) of Advocate were issued to them. Chhatrapati sent Khabade, Chopade, Karvekar and others from depressed classes to Mission Hospital at Miraj for the course of medicine and also helped them in opening the dispensary. Some persons were sent to Bombay for the training of haircutting and tailoring jobs.

They were given help for opening of their shops by giving clothes of the palace-servants for stitching. Then other caste-Hindus also started giving their clothes to them. Chhatrapati encouraged and supported Gangaram Kamble, a Mahar, to open a hotel at the gate of the palace. Shahu himself was going to that hotel for tea, and other officers who were accompanied had to follow him. Gangaram was maintaining it neat and clean. Some caste-Hindus also had started going to his hotel. In this way, Shahu's educational-professional policies and programmes proved to be useful and encouraging for the elevation of ex-untouchables' status.

Appointments in Palace and State Administration

To keep the balance of power and encouraging the Backward Classes, Shahu Chhatrapati trained many men from the non-Brahmin community down to the ex-untouchables and appointed them in the palace and the State Administrative services. Accordingly, he appointed many from Mahars, Mangs, Dhors and Chambhars for his household services and the State services.

Some dog-keepers, hunters of birds and animals were appointed from Mangs at his palace. His Highness appointed some persons from ex-untouchable castes as drivers on the motors of Chhatrapati's kins. Yallappa Naik, a Mahar was driver on Shahu's motor. Some were appointed as chariot drivers. Many men from Mahar community were given the jobs of postmen and coachmen. Bodyguards to Maharaja were mostly from depressed classes. Many peons, police and attendants were appointed from ex-untouchable castes. Uneducated ex-untouchable men were used in Shahu's household services. Men who were placed on the coach-boxes of State carriages were brought before public through visible occasions such as marriage, so that upper Caste-Hindus would not look down upon them. Some men from Mahars and Mangs were placed on an elephant, an animal was considered a privilege of royal family only. To become an elephant-rider, was regarded a matter of pride. A sword also was considered a privilege of warrior caste. Ex-untouchable men with swords and belts were brought before the public on ceremonial occasions.

In 1919, by the order of His Highness appointments of R.S. Kamble, D.S. Powar, and D.R. Vhatkar were made in the accounts branch office, in the chief police office and in the forest office respectively. Some men from depressed classes were appointed as talathis. By order of dt. 16.1.1919 some men from the same depressed classes were appointed and promoted as clerks. Shahu had adopted merit promotion scheme also and accordingly the preference was given to the depressed class men for promotions in their positions in every department of the State.

Programmes for Removal of Caste-Disabilities of Ex-Untouchables

By issuing orders as and when required, Shahu had abolished untouchability in the various Departments of the State. A practice of daily roll-call of ex-untouchables to the village officers was put to an end. Moreover, Chhatrapati appealed Mahars to give up their pieces of land and shift towards self-employed occupations. In response to the call, some Mahars showed their readiness by application of dt. 27.7.1921 and thus, the practice of forced labour was seemed to be on waning.[4]

Untouchability was not only removed merely by issuing the orders but Chhatrapati had removed it first from his personal life also. It is well known fact that Shahu Chhatrapati was used to drink and eat from the hands of the ex-untouchables. Whenever he had to go out of his State, he was moving with those people and was drinking and eating in the company of those. Once he went to segregated quarters of the Mahars and called out a Mahar for water and drank it before the crowd assembled around him. The Maharaj had a hobby of hunting . While going out for hunting he was eating his food from the tiffin kept with the Mahar servant. Once he did not bring his water and tiffin. He became thirsty and hungry. While moving in the jungle he saw a man with bread and water. He got it from him and ate it without enquiring his caste, but later came to know that the breads baked were from the home of a Mahar.

Chhatrapati was not only satisfied over his policies framed but he was after its fullest execution also. So he formed the Executive Committee of the workers, named Dakshin Maharashtra Satyaprasarak Mandal (South Maharashtra Truth Spreading Committee) to redress the grievances of depressed classes. In the context of execution of his orders, it would not be worth if a notable incident of Gangaram Kamble is not mentioned. Once, after eating mid-day bread Gangaram Kamble, a Mahar servant of the palace drank water from the tap of a cistern. As he dared to do so, he was beaten by the upper caste-Hindu servants. Shahu Maharaj came to know of the incident. He visited the spot. He summoned the men who had beaten Gangaram and punished them.

Motivation to Social Workers

When Dr. Ambedkar became M.A., Ph.D. and returned from foreign study, Shahu Chhatrapati personally went to him at his Parel residence in Bombay to congratulate and embrace him. There itself he was given invitation to come to Kolhapur. Dr. Ambedkar in Kolhapur was honoured by offering a Kolhapuri turban by Chhatrapati himself and suggested him to fight against injustices and to work for the depressed classes. Later on, in 1920 Dr. Ambedkar presided over the first Congress of the Deccan Untouchables in the presence of Shahu at Mangao. In the same conference Shahu predicted that Dr. Ambedkar will be the leader of the untouchables and the nation as well. Since the moment Dr. Ambedkar became inspiration to the Dalits of Kolhapur and outside also.

Shahu not only appreciated Dr. Ambedkar but encouraged and also supported other workers from ex-untouchable groups to educate their brethren and to make them aware of their rights. Shahu had appointed Mr. Gangaram Kamble as a social worker. He had asserted first his right by entering the hotel of Mr. Mane in Bindu Chowk of Kolhapur when the ex-untouchables had no entry into it. Also he had asserted first similar right to take water from the public tap. He had taken initiative to occur intercaste marriage between a boy from the Lingayat caste and a girl from the Mahar caste. Under the guidance of Dr. Ambedkar an association of Depressed people was established in Kolhapur and a Conference was held in 1939 under the presidential chair of Dr. Ambedkar. Some other notable workers can be mentioned here. Mr. D.S. Powar, a Chamar who was made Chairman of the Standing Committee of Kolhapur Municipality by Chhatrapati and then Sub-divisional Magistrate and M.L.A., and Mr. D.D. Gholap, a Mahar representative of ex-untouchables in Bombay Legislative Council in 1924, was given educational help by Shahu. Mr. K.L. More, a Mang who had become a member of various public bodies, viz., the Education Committee, the Panchayat Committee, the Kolhapur Municipal Council, the Kolhapur Legislative Assembly, twice elected member of Parliament and an advocate of Supreme Court, was admitted student by Shahu in Gurukul (residential) School. All these workers and later political leaders were given help by Shahu in their life-career.

Inducement to Mixed Locality

The pattern of locality settlement of Indian village is developed on caste line and the same is true of town or city also, however, lesser in degree. It has been one of the characteristic features of the Indian community that ordinarily a person wanted to live in a locality of caste to which he belongs. Even nowadays, in a housing society, a member is preferred either from own caste or closer to own caste. In such a background, Shahu started to give housing accommodation in the midst of caste-Hindus' locality. A house was given to Dashrath Sakate, a dog-keeper from a Mang caste in Shahupuri in Kolhapur town. Shahu had told the ex-untouchables to set on fire their localities of outskirt so that the plots for housing would be made available in the heart of the town. It indicates Shahu's strong motivation for the elevation of ex-untouchable groups.

Temple Entry

Dr. Ambedkar and his brethren launched a campaign for temple entry but they failed to get entry. Shahu Maharaj had opened his Bhawani temple for all including the ex-untouchables.

Suggestion to Adopt the Maratha-Brahmin Surnames

Naming pattern in caste system is one of the characteristic features of caste identities. In order to change such caste identity, Shahu had advised ex-untouchables to adopt the surnames of the upper caste-Hindus.[5] Chhatrapati himself took a step to address the wrestlers as Jat, Sardar and Pandit from Mahar, Chamar and Bhangi respectively. During his time no body could become ready for wrestling with an ex-untouchable wrestler. Shahu himself belonged to Suryawanshi clan and so he had addressed some men by Suryawanshi surname. In this way, the pattern of changing surnames was accepted.

Thus, Shahu Maharaj did his best for the removal of caste-disabilities of ex-untouchables through special efforts for elevation from their low status by providing opportunities in the schools, in the State administration, and in political power.

Role of Dr. Babasaheb Ambedkar

For the improvement of ex-untouchable people in their living habits, Dr. Ambedkar had emphasized on abandoning of old food habits of eating beef and carcass, and unclean living. The resolution relating dirty habits and customs to be stopped by the ex-untouchables, was passed in the ex-Untouchables' Conference of Mahad Satyagraha in 1927, and the same resolution was published in the periodical of 'Bahishkrit Bharat'. Dr. Ambedkar had started a campaign among the ex-untouchables to give up dirty habits. As a result of his campaign the Mahars of Colaba and Ratnagiri districts had given up the eating of meat of dead animals.

The different aims of ex-untouchables' Movement led by Dr. Ambedkar can be outlined as under:

First is, to remove untouchability and to secure equal rights for untouchable people as caste-Hindus enjoy.[6] For the removal of untouchability, he wanted to bring about social revolution through religious conversion. Accordingly, he embraced Buddhism at Nagpur on 14th October, 1956. He voiced 'struggle for equality' as one of his objectives. According to him, 'equality can be achieved only when intercaste marriages and inter-caste dinners take place freely' and it is possible by adopting the path of conversion.

Second is, to secure political power for the representation in the Legislatures of the country. The objective of political representation in the Council Hall was to fight for the redress of their grievances. He held that the problems of the Depressed Classes will never be solved unless they get political power in their own hands. Dr. Ambedkar being the President of Depressed Classes Institute established in June 1925 with the aim: 'to raise the Depressed Classes from the present day downtrodden condition to a status of social and political equality in Indian society and to promote their economic welfare'. 'Our struggle is only for political power' was expressed by Dr. Ambedkar in his speech delivered at Wadala, Bombay on dt. 5.9.1932. All it suggests his emphasis on securing political power. Therefore, the instrument 'Republican Party of India' given by Dr. Ambedkar is used for power politics by his ex-untouchable brethren.

Third is, to enter the public services for securing power and control over the administration. For entry in Government, Dr. Ambedkar's call to the ex-untouchable masses is popular by his slogan: 'Educate, Organise and Agitate'. The aim of securing political and administrative power was to secure equal rights ultimately.

To sum up, the present Dalit movement which is known for their militancy and agitating actions is the impact of Dr. Ambedkar's motivation chiefly. Rise of self-respect notion especially among the Mahars and consequently among the other ex-untouchable castes people is, in fact, an impact of Dr. Ambedkar's movement.

To conclude the role of social reformers in Maharashtra, that, it has influenced the awakening of ex-untouchables of their low status and it has also influenced the upper caste-Hindus' conscious of their responsibility towards the removal of untouchability and their emancipation through access in power positions and different professions.

NOTES AND REFERENCES

1. Stated in written memoirs of Mahatma Jotirao Phule by Govind Ganpat Kale; See, Purogami Satya Shodhak (Marathi Quart.), Mahatma Jotirao Phule Samata Pratishthan, 1212, Bhavani Peth, Pune, Nos. 3-4, July-Dec., 1981, p. 14.
2. Latthe, A.B.: Memoirs of H.H. Chhatrapati Shahu Maharaj of Kolhapur, 1924, pp. 484-86.
3. Ibid., p. 572.
4. Sanad issued by Shahu Chhatrapati is an evidence. True copy of the Sanad is attached herewith.
5. It is evidenced from the Sanad issued by Shahu.
6. It is evidenced by the name of organization itself, i.e., Samaj Samata Sangha (Social Equality League) established on dt. 4.9.1927 by Dr. Ambedkar.

Sanad Issued by Shahu Chhatrapati to Mr. Baburao Kamble

The important features of the Document issued by Shahu Maharaja in 1920, to Baburao Kamble (Mahar), are laid down as under:

(1) The Mahars were made slaves and they were treated inhumanly inspite of their honest services to the village people. It is the responsibility during the present period of reformation to make them free from slavery by giving education.

(2) The Mahars unanimously agreed to become free from village slavery, so the sixteen Mahars are given appointment in the State services.

(3) The surnames such as Kale, Sarnaik, Banage, Ligade are not original but attached by Shahu Maharaj as per his advise to 'change surname' so as to become free from caste identification.

(4) They shall be treated as officers of the State. They will not be told any household work.

(5) His Highness the Chhatrapati Shahu is confident of their status elevation by educating their generation.

A original copy of the Document is issued in Marathi language. The text is attached herewith.

स्वस्तिश्री राज्याभिषेक शके २४७ रौद्रनाम संवत्सरे वैशाख बद्दल १० दशमी रोज गुरुवासरे क्षात्रिय कुलावतंस श्रीमन्महाराज शाहूछत्रपति स्वामी यांनीं बाबूराव रामराव कांबळे यांस आज्ञा केली ऐसीजे:—

महार लोक गांवचे उत्पत्तीपासून आजपर्यंत गांवचे लोकांची व सरकारची इमानें इतबारें नोकरी करीत आले; परंतु आजपर्यंत त्यांना कोणीही उन्नतीचा मार्ग दाखविला नाहीं. नेहमीं त्यांना हीन स्थितीत व दास्यांत ठेवून अमानुषपणानें वागविल्याचें दिसून आलें आहे. अशा स्थितींत त्यांनीं आपलें इमान व राजनिष्ठा यत्किंचितसुद्धां ढळूं दिली नाहीं. ते मानवी प्राणी आहेत, व मनुष्याला मनुष्याप्रमाणें वागविण्याचें तत्वास अनुसरून सदर लोकांस दास्यापासून मुक्त करणें व त्यांना शिक्षण देऊन सुसंस्कृत करून श्रेष्ठ पदास पोंहचविणें हें हल्लींचे सुधारणेच्या काळांत आद्य व पवित्र कर्तव्य आहे, असें स्वामींनीं घ्यानीं आणून कसबा करवीर येथील महार लोकांस एकंदर उत्पन्न जमीन एकशे एकोणतीस एकर आठ गुंठे १२९।८ आकार रुपये चारशे सत्याणवर्ये

आहे. त्यास हल्लीं नंबर ९ चें कायदीं "समस्त महार" यांचे नांव दाखल आहे. तें महार लोकांनीं एक वाक्यतेनें कबुली दिल्यानें कमी करण्यांत येऊन सरकारीकामास सोळा इसम नेमून देण्याचें ठरविलें असून त्यांचीं नांवें खालीं दिलीं आहेत.

१ बाबूराव रामराव कांबळे	९ बाळाजी चोळाजी काळे
२ कृष्णराव परशराम कांबळे.	१० नाभू राणोजी काळे.
३ नागोजी तिपाजी कांबळे.	११ मसू मानाजी काळे.
४ रामू शंकर कोले.	१२ मसू लक्ष्मण काळे.
५ सदू तुकाराम वनगे.	१३ आवा जकू सरनाईक.
६ जोती नायकू वनगे.	१४ सदू राणोजी सरनाईक.
७ लिंबारी संतू लिगाडे.	१५ भाऊ तुळसा कालेकर.
८ जोती सुभाना लिगाडे.	१६ तुळसाप्पा संतराम सरनाईक.

या सोळा इसमांपैकीं तुह्मी एक असल्यानें तुह्मास करवीर येथील "समस्त महारांचें" जमीनींपैकीं आठ एकर तीन ८-३ गुंठे जमीन वंशपरंपरा नोकरी इनाम देण्यांत आली आहे. सरकारी नोकरीस नेमून दिलेले सोळा इसम जबाबदार रहातील. त्याप्रमाणें तुह्मी व तुमचे पुत्रपौत्रादि वंशज जबाबदार राहून स्वामीसेवा इमानें इतबारें व एक निष्ठेनें करावी.

तुमचे इनाम जमीनीस इतर इनाम जमीन धारण करणारे म्हणजे सनदी शिलेदार, कोटकरी व हुजूर सनदी वगैरे इसमास जें नियम लागू आहेत, तेच नियम लागू होतील.

नेमून दिलेल्या सोळा इसमानीं सरकारी नोकरी करण्याची आहे. खुद्द हुजूर स्वारी, आईसाहेब महाराज, युवराजमहाराज यांजकडे नोकरी करण्याची आहे. तसेंच पडल्यास त्यांनीं श्रीमहालक्ष्मी करवीर निवासिनीकडेही नोकरी करण्याची आहे. सरकारी टपाल व वर्दी करण्याची आहे. खुद्द राजघराण्यांतील पाकळे बंधु अगर पाकळे राजपुत्र व राजकन्या वगैरे त्यांचे वंशज यांचेकडे ही करण्याची नाहीं.

त्याचप्रमाणें रयतेच्या कामगाराची अगर अधिकाऱ्याची दिवाणापासून तहत गांवच्यां पाटलापर्यंत कोणाचीही नोकरी असली तरी त्यानी ती हकानें म्हणून करून घेण्याची नाहीं. त्यांनी पडेल ती मजूरी देऊन वाटेल त्या इसमाकडून करून घ्यावी मग तो मनुष्य हिंदु, मुसलमान, ब्राह्मण, महार, मांग, मराठा, जैन लिंगायत, कोणीही असो.

नोकरी करितां नमूद करून घेतले १९ इसमास सनदी शिलेदार व हुजरे यांचे दर्ज्याप्रमाणें वागविण्याचें आहे. त्यास गांवकामगार यांनीं कोणतेही घरगुती काम सांगण्याचें नाहीं.

नेमून दिले इसमास तसेंच तुम्हांस आतां भरपूर वेतन मिळालें असल्यानें आपआपल्या वंशजाची उन्नती करून घेण्यास सुलभ मार्ग करण्यांत आला आहे, तरी ते आपली पिढी सुशिक्षित करून श्रेष्ठ पदास पोंचतील असा स्वामीस पूर्ण भरंवसा वाटत आहे.

महार लोकांची संख्या सरकारी नोकरीसाठीं मर्यादित करण्याकरितां स्वामीनीं ही योजना केली आहे. तरी या पुढें आजवरच्या अनिष्ट चालीनें गलिच्छ कामासाठीं अगर वेठ बरला करण्यासाठीं महार ज्ञातीचें लहानापासून ते थोरा पर्यंत सर्व स्त्री पुरुषास वतनी बंधनास चिकटून राहावें लागणार नाहीं. त्यांचे उन्नतीचे मार्गांत असलेला हा अडथळा दूर करण्यांत आल्यानें त्यांच्या खऱ्या उन्नतीला लवकरच प्रारंभ होऊन मानवी प्राण्यांत त्यांची गणना चांगले पदास पोंहचेल अशी स्वामीस पूर्ण उमेद आहे. तरी तुम्ही व तुमचे पुत्रपौत्रादि स्वामी कार्य एकनिष्ठेनें करून आपलें वंशज सुशिक्षित करून घेण्यासाठीं स्वामीनीं कृपाळुपणें तुम्हास सुसंधी उदात्त हेतूनें दिली आहे. तरी तिचा उपयोग करून तुम्ही व तुमचें पुत्रपौत्रादी स्वामीसेवा उत्तम प्रकारें करून वंशपरंपरा जमीन अनुभवून सुखरूप राहणे जाणिजे.

APPENDIX III

Relevant Articles from the Constitution of India

14. Equality before law:

The State shall not deny to any person equality before the law or the equal protection of the laws within the territory of India.

15. Prohibition of discrimination on grounds of religion, race, caste, sex or place of birth:

(1) The State shall not discriminate against any citizen on grounds only of religion, race, caste, sex, place of birth or any of them.

(2) No citizen shall, on grounds only of religion, race, caste, sex, place of birth or any of them, be subject to any disability, liability, restriction or condition with regard to -

(a) access to shops, public restaurants, hotels and places of public entertainment; or

(b) the use of wells, tanks, bathing ghats, roads and places of public resort maintained wholly or partly out of State funds or dedicated to the use of the general public.

(4) Nothing in this article or in clause (2) of article 29 shall prevent the State from making any special provision for the advancement of any socially and educationally backward classes of citizens or for the Scheduled Castes and the Scheduled Tribes.

16. Equality of opportunity in matters of public employment:

(1) There shall be equality of opportunity for all citizens in matters relating to employment or appointment to any office under the State.

(2) No citizen shall, on grounds only of religion, race, caste, sex, descent, place of birth, residence or any of them, be ineligible for, or discriminated against in respect of any employment or office under the State.

(4) Nothing in this article shall prevent the State from making any provision for the reservation of appointments or posts in favour of any backward class of citizens which, in the opinion of the State, is not adequately represented in the services under the State.

17. Abolition of Untouchability:

"Untouchability" is abolished and its practice in any form is forbidden. The enforcement of any disability arising out of "Untouchability" shall be an offence punishable in accordance with law.

19. Right to freedom of occupation:

(1) All citizens shall have the right -

(g) to practise any profession, or to carry on any occupation, trade or business.

23. Right against exploitation:

(1) Traffic in human beings and beggar and other similar forms of forced labour are prohibited and any contravention of this provision shall be an offence punishable in accordance with law.

46. Promotion of educational and economic interests of Scheduled Castes:

The State shall promote with special care the educational and economic interests of the weaker sections of the people, and, in particular, of the Scheduled Castes and the Scheduled Tribes, and shall protect them from social injustice and all forms of exploitation.

330. Reservation of Seats for Scheduled Castes in the House of tne people.

(1) Seats shall be reserved in the House of the people for -
 (a) the Scheduled castes;
(2) The number of seats reserved in any State or Union Territory for the Scheduled Castes or the Scheduled Tribes under clause (1) shall bear, as nearly as may be, the same proportion to the total number of seats allotted to that State or Union Territory in the House of the People as the population of the Scheduled Tribes in the State or Union Territory or part of the State or Union Territory, as the case may be, in respect of which seats are so reserved, bears to the total population of the State or Union Territory.

332. Reservation of Seats for Scheduled Castes in the Legislative Assemblies of the States:

(1) Seats shall be reserved for the Scheduled Castes and the Scheduled Tribes, in the Legislative Assembly of every State.
(3) The number of seats reserved for the Scheduled Castes or the Scheduled Tribes in the Legislative Assembly of any State under clause (1) shall bear, as nearly as may be, the same proportion to the total number of seats in the Assembly as the population of the Scheduled Castes in the State.

335. Claims of Scheduled Castes to services and posts:

The claims of the members of the Scheduled Castes and the Scheduled Tribes shall be taken into consideration, consistently with the maintenance of efficiency of administration, in the making of appointments to services and posts in connection with the affairs of the Union or of a State.

338. Special Officer for Scheduled Castes:

(1) There shall be a Special Officer for the Scheduled Castes and Scheduled Tribes to be appointed by the President.

(2) It shall be the duty of the Special Officer to investigate all matters relating to the safeguards provided for the Scheduled Castes and Scheduled Tribes under this Constitution and report to the President upon the working of those safeguards at such intervals as the President may direct, and the President shall cause all such reports to be laid before each House of Parliament.

340. Appointment of a Commission to investigate the conditions of backward classes:

(1) The President may by order appoint a commission consisting of such persons as he thinks fit to investigate the conditions of socially and educationally backward classes within the territory of India and the difficulties under which they labour and to make recommendations as to the steps that should be taken by the Union or any State to remove such difficulties and to improve their condition and as to the grants that should be made for the purpose by the Union or any State and the conditions subject to which such grants should be made, and the order appointing such Commission shall define the procedure to be followed by the Commission.

(2) A Commission so appointed shall investigate the matters referred to them and present to the President a report setting out the facts as found by them and making such recommendations as they think proper.

(3) The President shall cause a copy of the report so presented together with a memorandum explaining the action thereon to be laid before each House of Parliament.

341. Scheduled Castes:

(1) The President may with respect to any State or Union Territory, and where it is a State, after consultation with the Governor thereof, by public notification, specify the castes, races or tribes or parts of groups within castes, races or tribes which shall for the purposes of this Constitution be deemed to be Scheduled Castes in relation to that State or Union Territory, as the case may be.

(2) Parliament may by law include in or exclude from the list of Scheduled Castes specified in a notification issued under clause (1) any caste, race or tribe or part of or group within any caste, race or tribe, but save as aforesaid a notification issued under the said clause shall not be varied by any subsequent notification.

366. Definition of Scheduled Castes:

(24) "Scheduled Castes" means such castes, races or tribes or parts of or groups within such castes, races or tribes as are deemed under article 341 to be Scheduled Castes for the purposes of this Constitution.

REFERENCE

1. Government of India: The Constitution of India (As modified upto the 15th August, 1983); Ministry of Law, Justice and Company Affairs, New Delhi.

APPENDIX-IV

A Brief History of Financing Agency: Mahatma Phule Backward Class Development Corporation[1]

The Government of Maharashtra has established 'Mahatma Phule Backward Class Development Corporation, on 10th July 1978 with an objective of supporting for occupational activities in the interests of Scheduled Castes, Neo-Buddhists, Scheduled and Nomadic Tribes people. In order to serve the objective, the Corporation has opened eight regional offices in the State of Maharashtra.

Objectives

The margin money is given to the applicant who is willing to start economic activity like production, trade, profession, agriculture, animal husbandry, fruit garden, dairy development, or any other. The objective of the loan distribution is to motivate to start the activity like agriculture and its allied, industry, village and cottage industries, transport and service activity etc.

Schemes of Loan Facilities

1. The 75 to 80 per cent loan of the required amount is to be sanctioned by the Bank and then the remaining 20 per cent of amount is to be sanctioned towards its margin money by the Corporation.

2. The Corporation gives loan upto Rs. 200 to purchase the share-capital of the Cooperative Society. There is another scheme of the Corporation to support 50 per cent subsidy and 50 per cent loan for ownership of the cycle-rickshaw.

3. The Corporation gives loan and subsidy upto Rs. 5,000 to start the profession of a doctor, an advocate, an engineer and architect.

4. The Corporation helps to attend the vocational training of short-term courses like dairy, poultry, tailoring, carpentry, weaving, plumbing, electrical, leather activity, etc. During the period of training the Corporation supports in the form of scholarship for lodging and boarding.

5. The Corporation supports to buy auto-rickshaw. For this, the Corporation pays advance amount monthly to the distributing agent for ten autorickshaws and the same is allotted to the needy applicants according to the rules and priority basis.

So far, the Corporation informs that it has given help in the form of loan for dairy development, animal husbandry, agricultural development, village and cottage industries, transportation, and services like sound, stationery, laundry, tailoring, firewood stall, tea stall, vegetable shop, grain-shop, grocery shop, etc.

Researcher is informed that the MPBCDC Regional Office is opened at Kolhapur in 1978. The trend-report of castewise (of five castes) and activitywise beneficiaries of the MPBCDC assistance given for the period of six months i.e., from 1st April to 30th September 1985 is stated below in Tables 1 and 2.[2]

TABLE 1: **Castewise Beneficiaries**

Sr. No	Caste category	No. of beneficiaries	Percentage
1	Mahar	110	29.24
2	Mang	69	18.21
3	Dhor	33	8.77
4	Chambhar	162	42.74
5	Bhangi	5	1.04
	Total	379	100.00

TABLE 2: **Activitywise Beneficiaries**

Sr. No.	Type of Activity	Caste Category					
		Mahar	Mang	Dhor	Cham-bhar	Bhangi	Total
1.	Speaker set, tyre repairing, mfgr. of plastic bags, chilly pounding machine, grinding machine, kerosene oil selling, locks repairing, scrap business and painting:	13	8	—	6	—	27
2.	Stalls & shops: firewood, tea, pan-bidi, coal, fruit, cycle, grain, grocery, utensils and clothes shop:	53	23	3	14	5	98
3.	Dairy, poultry, masala, sheep-goat, vegetable & chilly selling:	35	32	4	5	—	76
4.	Tailoring, bricks backing, waste paper, churmura-bhatti and zaari work:	4	1	—	2	—	07
5.	Shoe and coach making:	2	—	1	135	—	138
6.	Leather tanning:	—	—	24	—	—	24
7.	Rope and broom making:	—	3	—	—	—	03
8.	Load carrying on bullockcart:	3	2	1	—	—	06
	Total:	110	69	33	162	5	379

Note: For above mentioned activities, the range of loan is sanctioned from Rs. 1,000 to Rs. 5,000, and one half of the sanctioned amount is financed by the Bank as an obligation to the new 20-point programme of the Government of India towards loan and the remaining one half of the total amount is subsidised by the MPBCDC.

REFERENCES

1. Based on the published pamphlet (in Marathi) of the Mahatma Phule Backward Class Development Corporation (Government of Maharashtra Undertaking).
2. Register for 1984-85 beneficiaries of the MPBCDC, Regional Office, Kolhapur.

APPENDIX-V

A Brief History of the Development of Kolhapur Christain Mission with its Introductory Origin

Early History[1]

Mr. R.G. Wilder is the first missionary who was sent to Kolhapur in 1852 by the American Board of Commissioners for Foreign Missions to undertake mission work. His wife Eliza was co-worker with her husband in Kolhapur. Before proceeding to Kolhapur, on Oct. 25th 1852 Mr. Wilder had written for permission to the Political Agent of Kolhapur Native State. Mr. Wilder had specified the object of missionary work that it would undertake the work of the simple preaching of the Gospel to the voluntary hearers in the interest of the intellectual, moral and religious well-being of the native inhabitants. And, it would extend its work for the free-school service. On Nov. 20th 1852 Major Graham, the Political Superintendent of Kolhapur State had replied that the Government had no objection to begin mission work in Kolhapur. On the receipt of such reply Mr. and Mrs. Wilder had arrived to Kolhapur on December 4, 1852. On the day of their arrival, the Brahmins had sent a petition to the Government that they be banished from the State. The petition was forwarded to the Bombay Government. And, "the Bombay Government notified the Maharaja that Christian missionaries must be accorded the same rights in the State as it were given to the members of other religions. Hence, the reply ended with the words: 'The time to banish missionaries has gone by'."

Despite the Brahmins' opposition and persecution by them during 1861 to 1869 they worked as the only Christian missionaries preaching in 2,156 villages; and leaving a copy of the Bible or a Gospel in each village.

Work of Early Missionaries

1. *School Work*: When Mr. and Mrs. Wilder came to Kolhapur in 1852, there was only one school of twelve pupils in the entire city. Mrs. Wilder had opened the very first school for girls in the kingdom of Kolhapur in the old palace in 1853. There were 500 boys in Mr. Wilder's schools in the year 1855-1856, among the pupils was a nephew of the Maharaja, and the three others were from the palace. During 1861 to 1869 Mr. and Mrs. Wilder had 3,300 pupils in their schools, and 500 of these were girls.

2. *Conversion Work*: There were no converts for the first four years, but in the early part of 1857 two people were baptized. The first was a Maratha, who was bapt ized on 5th April, 1857. The second was Savitribai, of the Mahar caste, who was baptized on 26th April, 1857.

3. *Medical Work*: Medical work was begun at Panhala in 1880. The need for this work was emphasized. The American Mission Board had sent Dr. Wanless for such work. The Mission had selected Miraj. A site was secured and the building was completed in 1894. Dr. Wanless moved to Miraj in 1892. In 1899 an Annex to the Hospital was built. The Medical School was opened in 1897.

4. *Agricultural and Industrial Work*: Along the lines of primary schools and high schools, the Agricultural work was begin at Sangli. Also, the Industrial School was opened in 1913, and at Kolhapur in 1925.

At present, the expansion of the different institutional work of the missionaries can be enlisted:

A. Medical Institutions[2]

1. Mary Wanless Hospital, Kolhapur.
2. Lafayette Hospital, Nipani.
3. Wilson Memorial Hospital, Kodoli.
4. Sangli Health Centre, Sangli.
5. Wanless T.B. Sanatorium, Wanlesswadi.
6. Wanless Hospital, Miraj.

B. Educational Institutions[3]

1. Indumati Girls and Boys Hostel, Kolhapur.

2. Cameron School, Miraj.
3. Esther Patton High School, Kolhapur.
4. Esther Patton Primary School, Kolhapur.
5. Gram Sevak Shala, Nipani.
6. Gram Sevak Shala Hostel, Nipani.
7. Irwin High School, Kolhapur.
8. Kodoli Community Middle School, Kodoli (Dist. Kolhapur).
9. Kodoli Community Middle School Hostel, Kodoli (Dist. Kolhapur).
10. Sangli Kindergarten and Primary School, Sangli.
11. Sangli Industrial School, Sangli.

C. Churches in the Kolhapur Region[4]

1. Grace Memorial Church, Islampur.
2. Howard Church, Yede-Nipani.
3. Yellur Church, Yellur.
4. Aitawade Church, Aitawade.
5. Wilder Memorial Church, Kolhapur.
6. Kini Church, Kini.
7. Porle Church, Porle.
8. Vadgaon Church, Vadgaon.
9. Shiroli Church, Shiroli.
10. Miraj Christian Church, Miraj.
11. Soni Church, Soni.
12. Updegraff Memorial Church, Nipani.
13. Bedkihal Church, Bedkihal.
14. Sangli Church, Sangli.
15. Digraj Church, Digraj.
16. Kawathe Piran Church, Kawathe Piran.
17. Kumbhoj Church, Kumbhoj.
18. Sawalaj Church, Sawalaj.
19. Umalwad Church, Umalwad.
20. Bethel Church, Wanlesswadi.
21. Simpson Memorial Church, Kapri.
22. Kodoli Church, Kodoli.
23. Borpadle Church, Borpadle.
24. Thanapude Church, Thanapude.
25. Marshall Memorial Church, Herla.
26. Flint Memorial Church, Mazgaon.

27. Groefsema Church, Rukadi.
28. Princeton Church, Wadinge.
29. Chokak Church, Chokak.
30. Malgaon Church, Malgaon.
31. Tanang Church, Tanang.
32. Shirgaon Church, Shirgaon.
33. Hamidwada Church, Hamidwada.
34. Ashta Church, Ashta.
35. Kawalapur Church, Kawalapur.
36. Kothali Church, Kothali.
37. Nimani Church, Nimani.
38. Yedrav Church, Yedrav.
39. Nez-Shivapuri Church, Nez-Shivapuri.
40. Haroli Church, Haroli.
41. Ichalkaranji Church, Ichalkaranji.
42. Shiye Church, Shiye.
43. Saint Mary's Church, Rangoli.
44. Saint Christoper Church, Rui.
45. Goodshepherd Church, Patan Kodoli

REFERENCES

1. *Western India Notes*, Vol. X, Nov. 1928. No. 2. Kolhapur Church Council, Kolhapur.
2. Kolhapur Church Council of the United Church of Northern India, Thirty-seventh Annual Meeting Report, 1961, p. 186.
3. Ibid., Thirty-sixth Annual Meeting Report. 1960.
4. Ibid., Thirty-seventh Annual Meeting Report, 1961, pp. 157-58. Sr. Nos. from 42 to 45 added from the source of information supplied by Rev. Panhalkar.

Bibliography

Books

Abercrombie, Nicholas; Hill, Stephen and Turner, Bryan S.: Dictionary of Sociology, Penguin, 1984.

Atkinson, J.W.: An Introduction to Motivation and Achievement, Winston-Wiley, 1974.

Bagade, D.R.: Shahu Maharaj aani Kayadekanu (Marathi); Padma Prakashan Sanstha, Kolhapur, 1982.

Bagal, Bhai Madhavrao (ed.): Khanderao Bagal Yanche Nivadak Lekh (Marathi); Publisher - 'Jivankalyan', The Kolhapur Sugar Mills Ltd., Kolhapur, 1976.

Bailey, F.G.: Caste and Economic Frontier; Manchester University Press, 1957.

Barber, Bernard: Social Stratification; Harcourt Brace and World, 1957.

Bendix, R. and Lipset, S.M. (ed.): Class, Status and Power, Free Press, 1966.

Bose, N.K.: The Structure of Hindu Society (trans.), Sangam Books, 1976.

Buhler, G.: The Laws of Manu; trans., Motilal Banarasidass, Delhi (Reprint), 1975.

Chitnis, Suma: Literacy and Educational Enrolment Among the Scheduled Castes of Maharashtra; Tata Institute of Social Sciences, Bombay-88, 1974.

Das, Bhagvan: Thus Spoke Ambedkar, Vol. IV, Ambedkar Sahitya Prakashan, Bangalore, 1980.

Desai, I.P.: Untouchability in Rural Gujarat; Popular Prakashan, Bombay, 1976.

Dumont, Louis: Homo Hierarchicus; Vikas Publications, 1970.

Dutt, N.K.: Origin and Growth of Caste in India, Vol. I, Mukhopadhyaya, 1968.

Galanter, Marc: Competing Equalities, Oxford, 1984.

Ganvir, Ratnakar (ed.): Dr. Babasaheb Ambedkaranche Bahiskrit Bharatatil Agralekh (Marathi), Ratnamitra Prakashan, Nagpur, 440004, 1985.

Gare, Govind and Limaye, Shirubhau: Maharashtratil Dalit-Shodh aani Bodh (Marathi); Sahaddhyayan Prakashan, Bombay, 1970.

Gavai, R.S.: The Scheduled Castes and the Scheduled Tribes and Their Service Privileges; Publisher; Kumbhare, General Secretary, RPI, Diksha Bhoomi, Nagpur-10, 1974.

Ghuge, V.B.: Chhatrapati Shahu's Socialistic Economic Policies; Kolhapur Zilla Parishad Publication, 1975.

Ghurye, G.S.: Caste and Race in India; Popular Prakashan, Bombay-7, 1961 and 1969.

Good, Carter V. (ed.): Dictionary of Education, 3rd edition, McGraw-Hill, 1973.

Hauser and Featherman: The Process of Stratification: Trends and Analysis; Academic Press, New York, 1977.

Ibbetson, Denzil Charles Jelf: Punjab Castes; Philadelphia, U.S.A., 1961.

Jadhav, Bhagvanrao Bapusaheb (ed.): Rajarshi Shahu Maharajanchi Bhashane (Marathi); Rajarshi Prakashan, Kolhapur, 1971.

Kamble, B.R. (ed.): Studies in Shivaji and His Times: Shivaji University, Kolhapur, 1982.

Keer, Dhananjaya: Shahu Chhatrapati - A Royal Revolutionary; Popular Prakashan, Bombay, 1976.

Khairmode, C.B.: Dr. Bhimrao Ramji Ambedkar (Marathi), Vol. III, Pratap Prakashan, Bombay-4, 1964.

—— Dr. Bhimrao Ramji Ambedkar Charitra (Marathi), Vol. IV, Dr. Ambedkar Education Society, Bombay-13, 1966.

Khan, Mumtaz Ali: Scheduled Castes and their status in India; Uppal Publishing House, New Delhi, 1980.

Latthe, A.B.: Memoirs of H.H. Chhatrapati Shahu Maharaj of Kolhapur, 1924.

Lakshmanna, C.: Caste Dynamics in Village India; Nachiketa, 1973.

Madan, G.R.: India's Social Transformation, Vol. I, Allied, New Delhi, 1979.

Mahar, J.M. (ed.): The Untouchables in Contemporary India; Arizona Press, Tucson, Arizona, 1972.

O'Malley, L.S.S.: Indian Caste Customs; Vikas, 1932.

Parsons, Talcott: The Social System; Routledge and Kegan Paul Ltd., London, 1970.

Patwardhan, Sunanda: Change Among India's Harijans; Orient Longman, 1973.

Peter, R.S.: The Concept of Motivation, Routledge and Kegan Paul, London, 1958.

Ransford, Edward H. and Jeffries, Vincent: Social Stratification – a multiple hierarchy approach; Allyn and Bacon, 1980.

Santhakumari, R.: Scheduled Caste and Welfare Measures; Classical Publishing Company, New Delhi.

Sarkar, Jayanta: Caste, Occupation and Change, B.R. Publishing, Delhi, 1984.

Shah, V.P. (ed.): Removal of Untouchability; Sociology Deptt., Gujarat University, Ahmedabad, 1980.

Sharma, K.L.: The Changing Rural Stratification System: Orient Longman, 1974.

Sharma, R.S.: Sudras In Ancient India; Motilal Banarasidass, Delhi, 1958.

Shyamlal: The Bhangis in transition; Inter-India, New Delhi, 1983.

Silverberg, James (ed.): Social Mobility in the Caste System in India; Mounton Publishers, The Hague, 1968.

Singer and Cohn (ed.): Structure and Change in Indian Society; Aldine, 1968.

Sorokin, P.A.: Social and Cultural Mobility, Free Press, 1964.

Suryawanshi, K.G.: Rajarshi Shahu Raja Va Manus (Marathi): Thokal Prakashan, Budhwar Peth, Pune, 1984.

Thapar, Romila (ed.): Indian Society: Historical Probings, Peoples Publishing House, 1974.

Tumin, Melvin M.: Social Stratification; Prentice-Hall India, New Delhi, 1981 (EEE).

Articles in Journals

Bopegamage, A.: 'Caste and Poverty', *Sociology and Social Research*, Vol. 57, October 1972.

Chekki, D.A.: 'Social Stratification and Trends of Social Mobility in Modern India', *The Indian Journal of Social Work*, Vol. 31, No. 4, January 1971.

Gangrade, K.D.: 'Social Mobility in India: a study of depressed class', *Man in India*, Vol. 55, 3 September 1975.

Goldthorpe, J.H. and Llewellyn, C.: 'Class Mobility: Intergenerational and Worklife Patterns', *The British Journal of Sociology*, Vol. 28, No. 3, September 1977.

Indiresan, Jayalakshmi and Gill, Shiela: 'Social Change Among Leather Artisans'; *Social Change*, Vol. 15, No. 1, March, 1985.

Jackson, E.F.; Fox, W.S. and Crockett Jr.: 'Religion and Occupational Achievement', *American Sociological Review*, Vol. 35, No. 1, 1970.

Kelley, Jonathan: 'Wealth and Family Background in the Occupational Career', *The British Journal of Sociology*, Vol. 29, No. 1, March, 1978.

Kerckhoff, A.C., Campbell, R.T. and Trott, J.M.: 'Dimensions of Educational and Occupational Attainment in Great Britain', *American Sociological Review*, Vol. 47, June, 1982.

Krausz, Ernest: 'Factors of Social Mobility in British Minority Groups', *The British Journal of Sociology*, Vol. 23, 1972.

Kulkarni, M.G.: 'The Scheduled Castes in Maharashtra: A Study in Social Change with particular reference to Mahars (Buddhists)', *Marathwada University Journal*, Vol. IX, July, 1969.

Kulkarni, M.G. and Hiramani, A.B.: 'Occupational Pattern in two Marathwada Villages - a comparative study', *Marathwada University Journal*, Vol. XIV, No. 2, September 1975.

Lapoint, E.C. and Lapoint, D.N.: 'Socio-Economic Mobility Among Village Harijans', *The Eastern Anthropologist*, Vol. 38, No. 1, Jan.-Feb. 1985.

Lieberson, S. and Fuguilt, G.V.: 'Negro-White Occupational Differences in the Absence of Discrimination', *American Journal of Sociology*, Vol. 73, No. 2, September 1967.

Lin, N. and Yauger, D.: 'The Process of Occupational Status Achievement', *American Journal of Sociology*, Vol. 81, No. 3, November 1975.

Mehra, Savita, Sharma, M.L. and Dak, T.M.: 'Changing Correspondence between Caste and Occupation: a socio-economic analysis', *The Eastern Anthropologist*, Vol. 37, No. 4, Oct.-Dec., 1984.

Parmar, Y.A.: 'Occupational Change Among Mahyavanshi–a scheduled caste', *The Indian Journal of Social Work*, Vol. XXXIX, October 1978.

—— 'Occupational Variation in a Scheduled Caste of Surat–A Case of Mahyavanshi', *South Gujarat University Journal*, Vol. X, 1981.

Phillips, W.S.K.: 'Social Structure and Mobility in an Urban Setting', *Social Action*, April-June, Vol. 30, No. 2, 1980.

Saberwal, S.: 'Receding Pollution: Intercaste Relations in Urban Punjab', *Sociological Bulletin*, Vol. 22, 1973.

Sharma, K.L.: 'Caste and Class: Factors Affecting Social Mobility Among the Scheduled Castes', *The Journal of Sociological Studies*, Vol. 2, Jan. 1983.

Singh, Soran: 'Occupational Mobility Among Scheduled Castes', *The Indian Journal of Social Work*, Vol. XXXVII, No. 3, October, 1976.

Singh, Kalam: 'Occupational Mobility in Rural Setting', *The Indian Journal of Social Research*, Vol. XXV, No. 2, 1984.

Treiman, Donald J. and Terrell, Kermit: 'The Process of Status Attainment in the United States and Great Britain', *American Journal of Sociology*, Vol. 81, No. 3, 1975.

Vidyarthi, L.P.: 'Position and Problems of Scheduled Castes in Bihar', *The Eastern Anthropologist*, Vol. 37, No. 3, July-Sept. 1984.

Yamaguchi, Kazuo: 'The Structure of Intergenerational Occupational Mobility: Generality and Specificity in Resources, Channels, and Barriers', *American Journal of Sociology*, Jan. 1983, Vol. 88, No. 4.

Periodical Sources

Alexander, K.C.: 'Changing Status of Pulaya Harijans of Kerala'; *Economic and Political Weekly*, Special Number, July 1968.

Karve, Irawati: 'What is Caste?; Caste and Occupations'; *The Economic Weekly*, Vol. X, No.. 12, 1958.

Nijhawan, N.K.: 'Occupational Mobility and Political Development'; *Economic and Political Weekly*, Annual Number, Vol. VI, January 1971.

Government Publications

Government of India

Census of India 1961, Vol. X - Maharashtra, Part V-A, Scheduled Caste and Scheduled Tribes in Maharashtra - Tables, Manager of Publications, Delhi-8.

Census of India 1961, Vol. X, Maharashtra, Part X (2-12), Cities of Maharashtra Census Tables.

Census of India 1971, Series-11, Maharashtra, Part-II-C(i) Social and Cultural Tables.

Census of India 1981, Series-I, India, Part II B[i], Primary Census Abstract, General Population.

Census of India 1981, Series-I, Part B(ii)_; Primary Census Abstract for Scheduled Castes; Registrar General and Census Commissioner, India.

Census of India 1981, Series-12, Maharashtra, Part-II-A, General Population Tables.

Census of India 1981, Series-12, Maharashtra, Part-II-B, Primary Census Abstract.

Census of India 1981, Series-12, Maharashtra, Paper 1 of 1981, Supplement.

Census of India 1981, Series-12, Maharashtra, Part-2 of 1982, Primary Census Abstract, Scheduled Castes and Scheduled Tribes, Director of Census Operations, Maharashtra, Bombay.

Report of the Commission for Scheduled Castes and Scheduled Tribes (July 1978-March 1979); Controller of Publications, Delhi-54, 1980.

Shiksha Paribhasha Kosh, Ministry of Education and Social Welfare, 1978.

The Constitution of India (As modified upto the 15th August 1983); Ministry of Law, Justice and Company Affairs, New Delhi.

Government of Maharashtra

Dr. Babasaheb Ambedkar: Writings and Speeches, Vol. I, 1979.

Dr. Babasaheb Ambedkar: Writings and Speeches, Vol. II, 1982.

Industrial Directory of Maharashtra 1979; Pune Division, Directorate of Industries, 1981.

Mahatma Phule Backward Class Development Corporation (Pamphlet in Marathi).

Salunkhe, P.B. (ed.): Rajarshi Shahu Gaurav Grantha (Marathi); Education Department, 1976.

Shinde, Maharshi Vitthal Ramji: Bharatiya Asprushyatecha Prashna (Marathi), 1976.

Vocational Survey of Kolhapur District; Education, Employment and Youth Services Department, Bombay, 1980.

Monthly, Weekly And Newspapers

Bahujan Nayak (Marathi), Nagpur, dt. 22.4.1984.
Economic Times, Bombay, dt. 14.12.1980.
Indian Express, Bombay, dt. 18.5.1984.
India Today, April 15, 1985.
Kurukshetra, New Delhi, April 16, 1977.
Manohar (Marathi), Pune, October 22-28, 1978.
Pudhari (Marathi Daily), Kolhapur, dt. 7.2.1983.
Purogami Satyashodhak (Marathi quarterly), Issues dt. 4.12.1977, Nos. 3-4 (July-Dec. 1981); Mahatma Jotirao Phule Samata Pratishthan, 1212, Bhavani Peth, Pune.

Unpublished Sources

Kamble, N.D.: Atrocities on Scheduled Castes in Post-Independent India; Institute of Social and Economic Change, Bangalore (Typescript)
Karveer State Gazette, 1919, Part I and Part 4; Department of Archives, Kolhapur.
Rahate, J.V.: Modernization Among Scheduled Castes With Special Reference to Mahars, Weavers and Sweepers of Nagpur City (Marathi); Ph.D. dissertation, Marathwada University, Aurangabad, 1985.
Sharma, Satish Kumar: Traditional Occupational Skills and Social Mobility; Paper presented in XVII All India Sociological Conference held at Surat, 1984.

Other Sources

Jagdale, S.S.: Asstt. Labour Welfare Officer, Shri Shahu Chhatrapati Spinning and Weaving Mills, Kolhapur for the figure of workers in the Mills.

Kulkarni, V.N.: Clerk of Bar Library, The Court of Kolhapur for the figure of Advocates.

Mohite, C.A.: Licence Superintendent, Kolhapur Corporation for the figures of the professionals in the City.

Regional Transport Office, Kolhapur for the population of Vehicles.

Register for 1984-85 beneficiaries of the Mahatma Phule Backward Class Development Corporation, Regional Office, Kolhapur.

State Bank of India, Kolhapur (Main Branch), the concerned officer supplied a copy of Bankers' Clearing House for the figure of the branches of Banks in Kolhapur city.

Sulgaokar (Dr.), Secretary, Medical Association, Kolhapur for the figure of Medical Practitioners and consultants in Kolhapur city.

Thirty-Seventh Annual Meeting Report (1960 and 1961) of Kolhapur Church Council of the United Church of Northern India, Kolhapur.

Twenty-Third Annual Report (1984-85) of Kolhapur District Cooperative Milk Producers' Society Ltd., Kolhapur.

Vhatakar, G.: Architect Engineer for the figure of Architect Practitioners in Kolhapur City.

Walikhindi, C.A.: Tax Practitioner for the figure of Tax Consultants in Kolhapur City.

Western India Notes; Vol. X, No. 2, Nov. 1928, Kolhapur Church Council, Kolhapur.

Western India Notes; Vol. XLVII, No. 2, April 1964, Kolhapur Church Council, Kolhapur.

Yadav, P.W.: Marketing Officer, Kolhapur District Cooperative Milk Producers' Society Ltd., Kolhapur for the figure of private and cooperative milk distributors in Kolhapur city.

Index